MARKETING OF SEEDS

MARKETING OF SEEDS

Editor
Premjit Sharma

2022
Gene-Tech Books

ISBN10 81-89729-87-X
ISBN13 978-81-89729-87-5

Published by : **GENE-TECH BOOKS**
4762-63/23, Ansari Road, Darya Ganj,
NEW DELHI - 110 002
Phone: 011-4300 3222
e-mail: genetechbooks@yahoo.co.in

PRINTED IN INDIA

Preface

The seed forms, literally as well as figuratively, the foundation of agricultural sector, and the burgeoning interest in plant science, seed science and technology has broken a whole new ground in the botanical world. Seed marketing forms a vital component of seed technology. Comprised of activities like acquisition and selling of packed seeds, intermediate storage, delivery and sales promotional activities, seed marketing is the crucial factor on which the size and scope of the seed industry depends.

Marketing of seeds is composed of the following essential parts: (a) demand forecast, which indicates the demand for a particular seed and its feasibility as per the season, (b) marketing structure or channel for distribution. In India, former to farmer seed distribution is done by cooperatives (c) Arrangement for distribution, i.e., transportational facilities (d) sales promotional (e) post sale service (i.e., technological help for the farmer), and (f) economics of seed production and seed prices.

This book has been written to facilitate the reader's knowledge with a thorough understanding of the growing seed industry. This fast developing sector has already been seeking attention as an important discipline of the agricultural process, and looks set to make new inroads into the same field. With a comprehensive but cruise exploration of the subject, it is hoped that the book would be highly useful for readers involved in agricultural science.

Premjit Sharma

Contents

1

Introduction

Seed marketing is one of the key component in seed industry which protects the interest of plant variety originating institute, seed producers, distributors and farmers as well. Seed marketing involves to make the business sustainable and rewarding. It needs a lot of promotional activities i.e. advertisement, public relations, brochures, sales aids, field days, seminars, demonstration plots and roadway signs. Therefore, seeds of improved crop varieties should be of the good quality and available at the right time in a sufficient quantity. The basic requirements for a stable seed industry capable of supplying seed for market demands must be ascertained:

1. An adequate supply of pre-basic and basic seed.
2. An efficient and strict certification system.
3. Reliable market intelligence to predict demand of cultivars.
4. Seed processing facilities near to seed production area.
5. Storage facilities available with distribution agency.
6. Documentation system.
7. Registration system of dealership.

8. Promotional activities about the benefit of certified seed. The success of a distribution network depends largely on the selection of competent retail dealer.

Marketing Activities

Marketing is not just advertising, distribution or sales but an integrated management process involving employees at every level of a business. In larger companies marketing will usually form one of the four major management divisions:

- Research and Development,
- Production, and
- Administration and
- Finance.

Although the structure and the degree of specialisation will depend on the size of the organisation. In smaller organisations one person may perform several functions or there may be just one person responsible for marketing and sales. Marketing activities are traditionally divided on the basis of operational activities, such as sales and distribution, and marketing service activities which include advertising, promotion and market research. Some of the marketing activities are:

- *Market research and analysis*: It involves finding out about the seed market through studying the nature of the product, where and by whom it is needed, at which times of the year and why.
- *Forecasting*: It entails using marketing information for the purposes of planning and making sound business decisions, such as how many bags of seed will be sold and how much seed should be produced

- *New product development*: It requires the identification of possible new products (e.g. by plant breeding) or making improvements to existing products, such as by using seed treatments
- *Product sourcing*: Involves licensing varieties and sourcing seeds from own and third-party suppliers
- *Product management*: concentrates on developing and implementing marketing policy for a seed product or range of products
- *Advertising, Promotion and Public Relations*: aims to create product awareness, influence farmers' buying decisions, (PR) and build up a positive perception of the company
- *Sales order administration and dispatch*: involves receiving and processing orders, allocating stock and dispatching orders, and maintaining stock records
- *Stock control and quality assurance*: involves managing the inventory for each class of seed, crop and variety, to ensure maintenance of germination and vigour
- *Distribution and transport*: entails moving the seeds from the point of production to the point of sale
- *Sales and invoicing*: The process of making the actual sale and receiving payment for it, i.e. the end result of the marketing activity
- *Management information*: involves collating and interpreting sales information and other information as a basis for monitoring operations and planning future activities
- *Customer care*: involves after-sales service, dealing with complaints and maintaining customer loyalty

Marketing Mix

In considering the needs of their customers, companies must think in terms of the product itself, the price of the product and the place where the farmer needs it, while making sure that the existence of the product is known through effective promotion. These various components are described below.

Product

The product is the focus of marketing. Although many aspects of the product are not marketing responsibilities (such as plant breeding, seed production and processing), marketing is concerned with the product's attributes and what these mean to the farmer. Such factors include quality, appearance and performance.

Price

Price creates sales revenue and is therefore important in determining the total value of the sales made. Price is really determined by what farmers perceive as the value of seed of a particular variety. It is important to understand how farmers value seed as well as how much they are prepared to pay in relation to the benefit they expect to earn.

Place

The place factor deals with the various methods of transporting and storing seeds and then making them available to the farmer. Getting the product to the right place at the right time depends on the distribution system. The choice of distribution method will depend on market circumstances and the nature of both the seed and the farmer.

Promotion

Promotion is the business of communicating with and influencing the customer. Although the cost associated with promotion can be a significant element in the overall cost of a product, successful seed promotion increases sales so that costs are spread over a larger output. While increased promotional activity may be a response to competitor activity or a new product launch, it is important to maintain a constant flow of messages to the consumer as well as visibility in the market place.

Mix

Mix is an appropriate word to describe the marketing process as it is a blending of ingredients to fulfil a common purpose. Each ingredient is vitally important and each depends upon the other for its contribution. Different markets will require a different balance of ingredients. The mix should comprise:

- a time scale,
- a seed company must have a plan which indicates when it expects to achieve its objectives, both in the short, medium and long term,
- strategic elements,
- these will involve the overall development strategy of the company and require considerable judgment and expert) se; such decisions might involve the development of a new seed product range or a new distribution system,
- tactical or medium-term elements,
- the business environment requires constant monitoring; a company should have sufficient flexibility in order to react quickly to changing

market circumstances, e.g. in response to competitor activity, which may require changes in pricing and promotional strategies or amendments to marketing plans,

- short-term operational elements,
- these involve predictable everyday decisions such as contacts with customers, organising advertising and point of sale material, and planning distribution.

Apart from those elements which are under the control of management, there are also a number of environmental factors beyond the control of management. Some of these factors are:

- competition,
- the competitors' strengths and weaknesses,
- economic,
- inflation, interest rates, credit availability, commodity prices, taxation,
- legal,
- import regulations, seed laws, consumer protection legislation,
- demographic & geographic,
- regional differences, both physical and cultural,
- technological,
- mechanisation, quality requirements, breeding advances, computerisation,
- distribution,
- the appearance of new outlets, cooperative development, direct marketing.

Marketing Strategy

The seed marketing strategy is based on two important factors:

1. Seed demand.
2. Seed supply.

Seed Demand

The total quantum of seed requirement is assessed on the basis of acreage, seed rate and renewal rates. But the assessment of demand for high quality seed is rather difficult. In this case, seed extension and promotion system and credit facility play major role in increasing the demand of certified seed among the farming community.

Diffusion of new varieties on farmers field greatly depends on:

i. Agronomic superiority.
ii. Farmer's education.
iii. Relationship of cost and benefits.
iv. Type of crop.

The variety which have superior agronomic character often adopted soon by the farmers. Educated and progressive growers quickly adopts new varieties as compared to subsistent farmer. Therefore, increase yield must cover the extra price for the seed and induce the farmer to use high quality seed.

Seed replacement rate

Many farmers usually save seed from the subsequent harvest of their commercial crop. If the seed promotional activities are effective, then farmers, awareness for the quality seed of the new variety will be fast. In self pollinated crops, the farmer normally replace seeds after 2-3 years, in cross pollinated crops, 1-2 years and for hybrids every year.

Seed extension and promotion

Seed extension programme is an important component of seed marketing of improved varieties. Farmer is often convinced better by actual demonstration of certified seed crop and common farmer crop. In Pakistan, Agriculture Department in public sector is responsible for all type of agricultural extension activities. Unfortunately, in seed sector, no well elaborated extension programme exist in Agriculture Department.

Public and private seed sector agencies have not paid due attention in seed promotional activities like well documented publicity of quality seed, seed demonstration plots or seed melas, seed literature or any other relevant activities. Very nominal publicity through TV aids is carried out by only Punjab Seed Corporation at the on set of sowing season of wheat and cotton.

Credit facility

Many farmers do not use certified seed due to the reason that they can not afford to purchase. Effective and soft term credit facility by the banks will help the farmer to purchase seed and other inputs. Successful credit programme also need good advisory services for the use of quality seed as is being practiced by pesticides fertilisers companies for their products. It ensures the effective use of input for better crop yield. Good return in term of yield will help in easy return of loan.

Seed Supply

Seed should be produced in a area suitable for high

quality crop seed but it should not far from potential consumers. Seed supply system is based on effective marketing and transportation network. Good packing attract the attention of consumer. Storage is also an important factor in supply of seed at right time.

Under the seed supply, the seeds of various crops pass through different channels. Public sector and private sector seed agencies have their own seed dealers and sale depots. Pre-basic seed is produced by breeders and handed over to public sector agencies or private seed sector especially multinationals produce their own seed. Basic seed produced by the authorised seed agencies, are distributed to private sector seed companies and to registered seed growers.

Certified seed so produced is distributed or marketed by the seed companies either direct by their own sale depots or through their seed dealer network. Farmers buy this seed from the local seed dealer or some time from the village shop keepers.

Pricing Structure

The sale price of quality seeds is always higher as compared to grain because quality seed production is a highly technical and institutional activities. In case of hybrid, the price of seed are even many time more than self pollinated and cross pollinated crop seed variety. Although the cost of certified seed is the result of a number of interacting factors, but the following factors have direct bearing on the price of seed.

1. Production cost including all inputs etc.
2. Harvesting, threshing and processing.
3. Storage cost.
4. Transportation and local taxes if any.

5. Retailing incentive including premium to the seed grower.
6. Risk cost from procurement to marketing.
7. Import of seed i.e. vegetable, oilseeds, forage fodder.

Healthy competition between public and private sector and among a number of seed companies and dealers network may determine and ensure the fair prices for both the producer and consumer of seed. The seed pricing system is not very systematic. Various seed agencies both public and private seed companies work out, seed prices differently based upon their specific seed production and procurement circumstances and competition among each other based on demand and supply basis. However, imported seed has higher price than locally produced seed.

2

Seed Production by Farmers

Seed is an essential element in agricultural production. The term 'seed' includes here both generative and vegetative parts of plants that are used for multiplication. The comprehensive system of plant breeding, certified seed production and marketing, which has been developed in the industrial world, is referred to as the formal system. Others use the words conventional or organised seed supply. This is a vertically organised chain of activities leading to the use of certified seed of approved varieties and hybrids.

The farm size varies between countries and continents depending on the availability and tenure of land among other factors. The type of smallholder farming, whether subsistence or market oriented, depends on resources, markets and alternative more lucrative forms of employment away from the land. For most of these farmers, seed production is no different to grain production. A few specialise on crops and varieties chosen on the basis of demand and simplicity of production.

Smallholder farmers often use their own seeds or resort to their neighbours' or local markets. No effort is made to store seed from one season to the next if seed is readily available. The smaller the holding the less likely the farmer will store seeds and purchase is often left to a last-minute operation immediately prior to planting. The primary source for such material is a recognised local crop producer whose resultant crop seeds always perform reliably. This reputation within the community ensures that the "seed" receives the necessary care and attention during its production.

It is fair to say, however, that in the majority of cases "seed" represents left-over grain. Where a seed production system does exist it falls into a recognised pattern of opportunist or specialist activity. Opportunists note seasonal shortages and work accordingly. This may involve sowing extra areas suited to the farming system by inter- or relay-cropping, and then harvesting and storing surpluses, acting as intermediaries in the supply of seed and seedlings or even illegal cross-border trading.

Seed Production Techniques

Several stages in the crop cycle require attention if the crop is to be used for seed. Correct site selection, good crop establishment and management, together with careful harvest and storage of the seeds are essential to ensure quality. Seed production techniques differ from crop to crop. Crops that lend themselves to vegetative reproduction or transplanting also have different requirements. Hybrids do not lend themselves to farmer seed production, although many farmers do sow the produce. Species with breeding systems requiring cross-pollination are at great risk and may not produce seeds.

Seeds may also be lost during storage in unsuitable seed storage climates. Research has shown that the prime components of seed yield (shoot density, seed numbers and harvest recovery) are severely affected by weather and farming practices. The best seed crops are produced in unbroken periods of suitable radiation, temperature and rainfall for vegetative growth, favourable photo period and temperature for floral induction and calm dry weather during maturation and harvest. Grower facilities (storage, inputs, equipment and labour) coupled with timely technical competence and the temperament to recognise seed as seed and not grain is also vital.

For traditional crops most of this information and the required skill is handed down from generation to generation. Care must be taken when handling cross pollinating crops in order to minimise genetic contamination. Block production or varietal zoning within a given area is often attempted for isolation. This has achieved only varying degrees of success due to neighbouring farmers independence. Legislative support has helped enforce such activities. If time and space isolation is not possible wind flow direction and plant selection from the centre of crop plots are less suitable alternatives.

Successful establishment (seedling emergence) depends on a complex interaction involving placement, size, genotype, seed characteristics (hardness) and the soil micro-environment. Farmers must ensure conditions favour germination, emergence and continued seedling growth. Local practices vary with season as well as with the crop, variety or the land. Climatic variables may also affect the seed crop but are generally beyond the control of the smallholder, unless fortunate enough to have access to for example irrigation facilities.

At planting, seed hardness is probably the characteristic most easily modified by the farmer. The seed can be soaked, scarified or cut to reduce hardness to a practical level of 40%. Access to inoculants is difficult. Rotating or introducing leguminous crops are the best practical means to overcome this problem. Recommendations as to crop establishment for seed production often indicate reduced plant populations but thereafter follow general cropping recommendations.

New crop variety introductions may change characteristics over two or three seasons as small scale, interested farmers continuously select from the seeds and the mother plants. Women are increasingly extending their traditional seed selector and keeper role. Selection of the mother plant now seems to be part of their mandate. Farmers require only a few plants, often hand picked, as seed for the next season.

Seed areas are seldom designated in the field. If so, they may change depending on crop appearance throughout the growing cycle. In many cases selection is by seed from the grain crop only. In vegetables the best produce is sold, the second best is consumed by the family and the worst left for seed! Thus a new introduction may differ considerably after only 1 season. Seed crop management is geared to maximise yield and quality. For crops with climbing, sprawling growth habits, additional possibilities exist through vertical production using support systems.

Crops with biennial and perennial life cycles will require appropriate seasonal renovation. They tie up land for considerable amounts of time and may therefore be seconded to less fertile areas, boundaries or bunds. The type of inflorescence will determine the harvesting technique. Dehiscence may delay or accelerate the operation by allowing material to be brushed or picked off the ground or harvested either as the whole plant or the seed bearing part for threshing and winnowing at the homestead or farm centre.

Small scale activities allow for manual harvesting and cleaning. This is more accurate, although time consuming. Improvements in output are still possible at the smallholder level, for example through use of scythes instead of sickles. Synchronised heading in all crops is recognised as vital but only experience and regular observation can really provide the basis for timing the harvesting operation. Simple examination of the inflorescence of the same small number of plants from flowering through to shattering will indicate the amount of time available for collection of seed to obtain optimum yield and quality.

Farmers are aware of the various techniques for delaying or improving operations according to weather or crop appearance. These techniques include stocking sheaves and manually rolling or winnowing standing crops. Post harvest operations are the activities that have been most dramatically mechanised. The scale of the operation determines the degree of mechanisation.

Seeds harvested from smallholder fields seldom have weed seeds in the sample (except for sprawling types), because the harvest technique leaves them behind. They do, however, often result in dirty samples because of threshing on earthen floors, which if adjacent to other seeds can result in varietal admixture. The crop and dirt admixture is easily picked out by hand. No machine can select and clean as well as the manual operation.

Seed cleaning focuses on winnowing and sieving/ selecting seed size. Local farm labour has done this since time immemorial. What has not been done, is the regular separation of seed from grain, unless the inflorescence (as in maize rice) can be stored as such. Simple winnowing by pedal driven or hand powered fans can complement natural wind. Enclosure in a box will allow concentration of effort in time and space. Smallholder storage is an area which still requires attention.

Crops and varieties traditionally suited to the tropics will naturally store better than crops suited to temperate conditions. Crops introduced under diversification policies may not store well. In these cases, small areas of farm land may have to carry the seed as a crop until the climatic conditions improve. Research has shown that drying seed to a hard bite test and sealing inside one or more layers of plastic of 480 microns thickness will help maintain quality during storage. The whole harvest should be stored in rat proof containers.

Traditional selection of cool storage locations should continue, as should the inclusion of local vegetative matter known for their insecticidal properties. Sometimes, however, tradition requires that these sealed units be reopened after/during the wet season for further drying. Local seed testing is not common. Petioles of bananas and aroids slit longitudinally can be used to wrap seeds for germination. A percentage of 80% plus is acceptable. A simple overnight soaking to verify the success or otherwise of hard seed treatment is seldom done.

The U.S national agricultural research systems (NARS) are expected to solve farmers problems. This frequently does not happen. Reasons vary from the absence of an operational extension research linkage to the NARS having a fixed programme which is unable to respond. Often there are simply insufficient resources available. Recent trends in the use of participatory rapid appraisal surveys (PRAS) by both NARS and the extension services have highlighted issues and farming practices previously unknown or considered not worth bothering about. They highlight farmer resourcefulness which should be harnessed to provide possibilities to develop more efficient technology.

Many research and extension reports show that most problems refer to inaccessibility of seed or poor emergence. The former concerns inadequate supplies or high prices from the formal sector, whether public or private, and may be compounded by frequent natural disasters. The latter refers to poor storage techniques. Such techniques may be adequate for "grain" but not for seed. The question of emergence must of course be put in context as the germination rates are seldom known. Genetic quality is seldom ranked as very problematic, presumably due to the regular selection by farmers.

Suitable solutions can be found to increase availability and seed quality either by research or information. Farmers are excellent communicators. They could be even better if the NARS and extension linkage and information services were improved. National, regional and international networking can assist in this area. The international agricultural research centres (IARC) are mandated to work with the NARS. Their involvement in adaptive research is limited but varies between institutes. Information exchange through formal linkages is already established.

CIAT and ICARDA seed production activities have been confined to the more formal seed programmes and the establishment of seed associations. Can the IARCS help the smallholders, who for the most part are independent of the formal seed system?

Financial Background of Seed Producing Farmers

Many governments, seed companies and in recent years an increasing number of non-governmental organisations (NGOs) have set up schemes to involve small farmers in seed production. Until recently, most schemes followed a more-or-less standard pattern. The small farmers involved are treated as contract growers. Thus, they are provided with source seed by the organiser of the scheme and are supervised in the production of a seed crop following formal field standards, usually laid down by the national seed certification authority.

The farmers involvement with the crop ends after harvest, when it is sold to the scheme organiser for a premium above prevailing grain prices. The organiser then takes responsibility for arranging the processing and certification of the seed, and its distribution—usually using a national input distribution network, either government- or company-run. Most of these schemes deal exclusively with seed of modern varieties (MVs).

There are numerous examples of this type of scheme in developing countries. The Ministry of Agriculture in Zambia runs its own scheme; the governments of Nepal and The Gambia have mandated NGOs working locally to assume responsibility for a substantial portion of national seed supply using smallholder seed growers. Increasingly, NGOs seeking to consolidate their rural development activities have started seed production projects based on this approach—often in areas where government and private sector services fail to reach. Examples include the Mennonite Central Committee's vegetable and soyabean seed schemes in Bangladesh, and the take-over of abandoned government seed facilities in Niassa Province, Mozambique by the Italian NGO Crocevia.

However, the performance record of this approach is mixed. As far as the local communities are concerned, the existence of the seed scheme may do little to improve seed supply in their immediate vicinity, because the seed is usually transported out of the area for processing and distributed using the national input distribution network, which may or may not cover the local area. Furthermore, scheme organisers tend to select the larger, better-resourced farmers as contract growers because they are able to comply with the exacting field standards that are required; the seed scheme therefore provides income opportunities only for a select portion of the community.

Within households, too, any benefits associated with the scheme tend to be directed to male members of the family. Seed crops are viewed as cash crops and are therefore usually a male preserve and scheme organisers tend to deal with male household members when handing over inputs, passing on production advice, etc. As regards the economics of this kind of conventional smallholder seed production, the evidence is that such schemes do not save costs compared to company seed farms or large-scale contract growers.

In Malawi, for example, the state marketing corporation found that it had to sell seed produced by smallholder growers at a loss. In fact, costs are often increased because higher levels of supervision are required, and dealing with large numbers of small growers adds to logistical costs for input delivery, field inspection and seed collection. In addition, there can be problems caused by the difficulty of ensuring the necessary isolation distances within a small farm community.

These costs are additional to the normal premium over grain prices that has to be paid to seed growers. At the same time, the demand for certified seed of modern varieties is relatively elastic with respect to price amongst the majority of farmers in developing countries. These are the 300 million farmers who operate in areas of comparatively low potential, which Chambers classifies as 'complex, diverse and risky' (CDR). These farmers tend to have limited resources of land and capital at their disposal and they are often unwilling to pay for MVs: seed is selected for its ultimate benefits (primarily increased or more secure production), so where MVs cannot provide these benefits—which is often the case in CDR areas—they will not be bought; and furthermore, even when there appear to be advantages to purchasing seed, households in CDR areas may not have the cash to pay for it.

Added to this, supplying seed to CDR areas is more expensive in terms of increased transport costs, supplying suitable varieties, and gathering the necessary information about households' preferences. All these factors result in there being significant imperfections in the market for seed produced by smallholder growers.

Alternative Farmer-based Seed Schemes

A growing number of NGOs are now experimenting with alternative farmer-based seed schemes derived from this kind of re-thinking. In Ethiopia, for example, the Canadian Unitarian Service Committee's Seeds of Survival Programme, in conjunction with the Ethiopian Plant Genetic Resources Centre, has organised multiplication of teff and sorghum seed using an adaptation of farmers' traditional seed systems. And since 1989 the Ecuadorian centre for agricultural services, CESA, has supported a similar scheme for potato seed multiplication and sale in local markets in the Ecuadorian Andes.

Some changes would need to be made if schemes made greater use of existing traditional seed systems within communities rather than copying formal sector production and distribution systems. Proximity of seed production and distribution is important. This emphasis on local level factors is not meant to suggest that greater use of traditional seed systems is a panacea, but failure to address these factors has led to failures in both conventional seed system development. Note that the precise economics of seed demand and supply varies between crops, depending on seed biology and also, importantly, on crop utilisation: what follows is only an outline of some of the principal points to be taken into account. These suggestions relate to generatively-propagated food crops, such as maize, beans and groundnuts.

In CDR areas, households want seed for a large number of different crops. They also want seed of various cultivars for each crop. It is now widely recognised that farmers select cultivars on the basis of criteria that go well beyond the yield potential envisioned in conventional plant breeding schemes.

Cultivars of different maturities are often required to accommodate early or late planting, variability in rainfall, or compatibility with intercrops or rotations; storage characteristics often assume greater importance for the farm household than for the plant breeder; local food preparation techniques and preferences often favour one cultivar over another; utilisation of non-grain biomass (leaves, stalks, etc.) for fodder, fuel or building material provide additional selection characteristics; and local crop markets may reflect a different set of demands from urban ones. These (and other) factors are not ethnographic curiosities but rather form part of the rigorous selection criteria that farmers use in accepting, or rejecting, seed of a new cultivar.

Not surprisingly, resource-poor farmers tend to demand relatively small quantities of seed. This is not only a function of land holding. We have seen that farmers often grow several cultivars of the same crop. In addition, most farmers attempt to save seed from one season to the next, in order to avoid cash expenditure. This is not to say that small farmers are not potential customers for good seed; Pray et al describe the widespread purchase of hybrid millet seed by small farmers in India for instance. But in general, seed replacement takes place less frequently than recommended.

Surveys in Zambia and Burundi respectively indicate that households typically seek to acquire no more than 10 kg of maize seed and 15 kg of bean seed per cropping season. Similarly, a survey carried out by Cromwell and Zambezi in Malawi reports typical quantities as being 5 kg for maize, 14 kg for groundnuts and 6 kg for beans. These amounts contrast to the standard pack sizes provided by conventional seed schemes, which are often sufficient to plant a hectare at recommended seeding rates. The pack size itself is cited as a significant disincentive to buying formal sector seed.

Formal seed schemes are now learning to package and distribute seed in smaller quantities, but this obviously adds to the cost. A more flexible system of accommodating small and variable demands for seed at the local level would have advantages.

Security of Supply

Farmers want to know that seed will be available when they need it. Judgements on when and what to plant are often made at the last minute. The rains may be early (or late), a first planting may have been lost to drought or pests, or a field or the equipment to prepare it may have become available at the last minute. Although it is often best to plant as early as possible, there are many unavoidable factors that cause delays, and farmers will be unlikely to tolerate the late arrival of seed as an additional burden. But this is often the situation in formal seed provision schemes, such as parastatals, with bureaucratic procedures for the allocation of vehicles and few incentives to encourage punctuality.

There are limits to the ability of any seed system to respond to the variable demands brought about by last-minute planting decisions, but proximity of supply is undoubtedly an advantage. In the Punjab of Pakistan, where most farmers obtain seed of new wheat varieties from other farmers rather than the seed depot, over half obtained seed in their own village and more than 80% travelled no more than 5 km in search of seed. Anything that can be done to favour more local level seed production will result in a saving for farmers. Transport costs are a major component of total seed production costs; cutting out the long-distance transport of seed from production site to distribution points would thus substantially reduce costs.

Another area where conventional smallholder seed production schemes could be changed concerns the typically strict adherence to seed 'regulatory frameworks'. By this we mean the set of seed laws, regulations, norms and standards that govern variety release and seed certification. We have already seen that the range of characteristics that farmers use in choosing varieties argues strongly for farmer participation in the varietal testing and release process. But laws and regulations that establish strict limits on the nature and quality of seed to be sold may also impose unneeded restrictions on farmer-based seed schemes.

Households in CDR areas do not want or need seed to meet all the standards that International Seed Testing

Association (ISTA) based certification systems provide; whilst the physical purity of seed and good germination percentages are valued, characteristics such as uniform seed size are often irrelevant. Except in certain environments where seed-borne diseases or off-season storage is a particular problem, the physical quality of seed sourced from small farmer seed systems is usually adequate.

Trials for farmer varieties collected in Zimbabwe show germination percentages of above 94 per cent for maize and 'higher than expected' for sorghum and millet. Genetic quality is also usually adequate, because a considerable amount of in-field roguing and post-harvest selection takes place. For self-pollinated crops, Heisey and Brennan report average yield losses from own-saved seed ranging from nil to 1.6 per cent per cropping season. Farmers' indigenous seed care skills and technologies thus appear to produce seed of equal or better quality to that produced by the formal seed sector.

At the same time, households are unwilling to pay for the additional cost of packed seed (packing seed is an integral component of formal sector seed certification schemes). Households will happily use seed from crops they have seen growing on neighbours' land, substituting 'neighbour certification' for formal seed certification, which unfortunately does not always guarantee high seed quality in any case.

Strict formal regulations on the type of seed offered for sale are meant to protect farmers, but if farmers have no access to either the legal system or to information on the exact source of the seed they are offered for sale, and if lack of resources at the state level means that the rules are either abandoned or followed strictly for a limited production of seed, farmers are not well served. There are now a number of examples of attempts to make the regulatory frameworks more flexible, ranging from mechanisms to allow farmers to have access to varieties before release (SADCC, nd) to proposals for more realistic alternatives to seed certification.

Seed Distribution

Another advantage of integrating seed production with distribution through schemes that build on existing traditional seed systems is that small farmer seed producers have access to a wide range of distribution modalities. They are often prepared to provide seed using exchange mechanisms other than cash. These include bartering for other commodities, labouring in return for seed, swopping seed of one variety for another, and gift giving based on social obligations. In many areas cash purchases or the use of credit are limited to the better-resourced households and the need to pay cash is cited frequently as a disincentive to the use of formal sector seed schemes.

Thus non-cash alternatives are an important means of giving a wide range of socio-economic groups access to seed. This is not to say that local seed distribution mechanisms function perfectly. Examples range from the wide search for new rice varieties in Sierra Leone described by Richards to the parochial characteristics of maize seed supply and varietal knowledge described by Friis-Hansen in Tanzania. But there is no doubt that when there are appropriate incentives, local level seed production can function and can expand to include complex networks that cover wide areas.

Social Equity in Seed Production

Modifying conventional smallholder seed production

schemes in the ways outlined above will not necessarily enable wider community participation in the income from seed production. Seed production requires time, land and knowledge—none of which are likely to be in the hands of the poorest. The social equity of traditional seed systems needs to be monitored carefully. The limited work that has been done suggests that this is influenced by the existing degree of social differentiation within communities and the nature of patron-client relations.

In some communities it may be more discriminatory than so far assumed. For example, access to seed may be limited to certain ethnic or social groups; or access mechanisms may perpetuate poverty through, for example, requiring large quantities of seed to be returned in payment for in-kind seed loans. In some areas, however, structures are more equitable. Muslim communities in Sudan and Mali have been documented as operating a seed tithe which is planted out in community seed plots. It is important to consider the specific seed needs of women farmers. In many areas, female-headed households form a significant proportion of the community.

Typically, relative to other households, they are short of labour and of cash and can therefore make only limited use of seed provided by formal sector schemes. Women within male-headed households are usually responsible for ensuring the domestic food needs of the household and they are particularly concerned with the storage, processing, cooking and organoleptic qualities of cultivars used by the household. However, these requirements are often relatively neglected by formal sector plant breeders who interface primarily with the male members of farming communities. It is important to ensure that alternative farmer-based seed production and distribution systems do not unduly transfer attention and resources away from women.

There is no moral hazard involved in obtaining seed through traditional seed systems, because households usually know the person supplying seed to them and often will have seen the crop from which the seed is supplied growing before harvest. Equally importantly, households are able to obtain seed of their preferred cultivars, which they know to be adapted to their particular production conditions. Individuals and households supplying seed charge lower prices because they do not face the additional transport, seed certification and information-sourcing costs of the formal sector seed suppliers.

Role of External Organisations

Too often, small farmers are already using low-cost systems of seed production, storage and distribution which produce good results but formal sector researchers and extension workers 'do not know about these practices and insist upon more sophisticated and costly methods'. They borrow unnecessarily from the organisational structures and quality standards of the formal sector, thereby incurring high costs and making it difficult for conventional smallholder seed production schemes to achieve economic viability in the long run.

For those agencies seeking to become involved in small farmer seed schemes, there is considerable scope for building on existing traditional structures for producing and distributing seed within the community rather than setting up new conventionally-organised smallholder schemes. This is often more likely to ensure the sustainability of the initiative in the long run. However, some modifications may be needed to ensure that seed reaches social groups without access to traditional community seed distribution mechanisms, such as certain ethnic groups, women farmers and poorer households. For example, a limited quantity of seed may be targeted on these groups by being distributed through other local development agencies working with them, such as church groups or health projects.

Linkages with institutions supplying extension services, complementary inputs, etc. are essential. It is important for external organisations to provide support for strengthening such linkages, which are often weak in CDR areas. A much longer time span of support is needed than many agencies currently anticipate.

Alternative farmer-based seed schemes may take at least ten years to develop to a degree where they are sustainable without outside support, even in favourable circumstances. Finally, organisations working with farmer-based seed schemes must recognise the significant influence on the economics of seed demand and supply of national-level policy decisions. Of particular importance are those relating to seed legislation, seed and grain pricing policy, and plant breeding the extent that the needs of farmers in CDR areas are catered for.

Integrated Seed Supply

Seed supply in developing countries has received considerable attention in agricultural development strategies since the 1960s. A wide range of seed projects has been launched since then. These projects have been built on the conception that every country can have a seed supply system which can be developed in a linear model in the way Douglas described. It is a simplification of reality to assume that these formal seed systems could be served by one blueprint development model in different countries. This is also true for seed supply within each country for a wide range of crops.

This widespread attention to the formation of formal seed supply systems in developing countries has resulted in a virtual denial of the existence of local seed supply systems. These consist of farmer selection, on-farm seed production and local diffusion. These activities are equivalent to breeding, production and marketing in the formal system. Since the farmer is primarily interested in the regular production of seed for his next planting and because selection and diffusion are not always equally important, the local seed systems can be considered horizontal.

These systems are also referred to as 'traditional', informal, or farmer-managed seed systems. There is never one seed system in any country, but seed supply is built on a number of dynamic processes of formal and local variety development and maintenance, and local and formal seed production and diffusion. These processes may vary in time and space. The importance of the formal sector is often grossly overestimated. From a farmer's point of view, seeds of optimum quality should be available at the right time and at an acceptable price.

The reliability of future supply can be an additional consideration. There are four components of seed quality; physiological, physical, sanitary and genetic. The first is related to germination capacity and vigour. Physical seed quality refers to the percentage of non-seed materials in a seed lot. Seed transmitted diseases affect the sanitary quality. Genetic quality refers to the value of the variety for cultivation and use, and is sometimes also related with the genetic homogeneity of a seed lot. Evaluation of different supply systems should thus consider these quality and availability aspects.

Formal Seed Supply System

The economy of scale of seed processing, research and production supervision in formal seed systems result in rather centralised large scale formal seed supply units. This arrangement allows for a strict control on physical, physiological and often also sanitary seed quality and on genetic identity. Whether the focus is on commercial or developmental aspects of seed supply, some level of economic returns have to be attained in order to reach an acceptable level of sustainability of the system.

Seed Quality

An important reason why the formal sector often fails to supply the majority of smallholder farmers is its inability to produce sufficiently adapted varieties (genetic quality of the seed). Breeders in the formal system, both in private and in public organisations have to select for wide adaptation of their varieties. Breeding of specifically adapted varieties would result in a wide range of varieties of which seed production is highly inefficient. Very poor contact between the 'scientific' breeders and their target groups often results in a total misconception of the needs of the latter, and in varieties that are not adopted by them.

A clear example is the long-time concentration of Malawian maize breeders on highly productive dent types, while the majority of farmers preferred the flint maize because of food storage problems. Numerous other examples of breeders' misconception have been documented and phrases like "the unwillingness of farmers to part with the old seed in exchange for improved seed" are still widely used. Even when farmers' needs are well understood, it can be very difficult to design an appropriate breeding programme.

Ceccarelli et al present some of the pitfalls of the selection of modern varieties for marginal conditions. Small farmers' preference for yield optimisation (stability) instead of maximisation has resulted in genetically variable land-races in the past. Improvement of these landraces through conventional breeding methodologies is very difficult and formal seed production and certification of the resulting genetically heterogeneous varieties virtually impossible.

Guaranteed seed quality through legislation and formal seed certification and quality control can be very effective to promote the production of high quality seed. It may, however, also adversely affect effective seed supply when bureaucratic variety release and seed quality control procedures are adopted. Seed legislation which is meant to protect the farmers can thus complicate farming.

Availability

The large investments in equipment and the necessary costs for research, marketing and managerial overheads necessarily raise the seed price well above the price of consumption grain. This factor is in general at least 1.8 times for self pollinated seeds (e.g. cereals, legumes) and up to 20 times for hybrids (e.g. maize). In the case of high value vegetable and flower seeds this ratio can be much higher. High cost of good quality seed can be acceptable when the returns for the farmer are high. Such high returns can generally only be expected in agro-ecologically high potential areas with good infrastructure and combined with good farming practices.

Seeds for mainly home consumed crops such as cassava and local vegetables are hardly ever bought from the formal sector. The cost involved in supplying a fragmented market generally results in a poor or total absence of seed supply to remote and resource-poor farmers and supply of 'small' crop seeds such as vegetables and local food crops like pigeon pea and cassava. This is especially true for crops where farmers can easily produce their own seed, such as self pollinated cereals and legumes.

Other supply factors include the timeliness and reliability of supply. This guarantee is especially vital in the supply of hybrid seeds but it is also important for other seeds. When farmers intend to purchase seeds they may not keep a security stock of home-produced seed, and when farmers rely on purchased seed for some time they may have lost important knowledge about how to produce and store seeds of these crops. Many—especially public—seed enterprises lack the necessary logistical expertise to guarantee the supply of good quality seed at the right time in all areas. Moreover public sector administrative procedures seriously hamper financial viability and thus sustainability of such formal seed systems.

Some major problems in formal seed supply in the public sector can be overcome or reduced by privatisation. Improved business management and more effective planning and logistics by private sector organisations can improve the reliability of supply and, especially in a non-monopolistic market, also seed quality. The scope of private seed companies is limited to supply of the most profitable seed crops to the commercially most interesting farmers. The consequence is often a reduction of the product mix and the range of farmers supplied.

Local Seed Supply Systems

Local seed systems are the predominant source of seed of

the majority of crop seeds in developing countries. In most cases, less than 10% of the total quantity used by farmers are supplied by the formal sector. Local seed selection has been the basis of domestication of wild and weedy species and the subsequent development of a wide range of land-races within crop species with high levels of adaptation to local agro-ecological and socio-economic conditions.

There are numerous examples of high levels of local knowledge with regard to varieties and seed selection. These apparent qualities of local seed supply mechanisms, combined with the experienced inability of the formal seed sector to supply large segments of the farming community has the risk of romanticising these local seed supply systems.

Seed Quality

The genetic seed quality referred to above is not always optimal for crop cultivation. Quickly changing needs of farmers due to intensification of agriculture or to soil depletion cannot always be catered for by the slow process of local and natural selection within genetically heterogeneous populations or by casual introduction of new material and local experimentation of new materials.

Farmers' practices can also lead to unintended selection for characters that are not preferred. Shallot growers in Bangladesh tend to plant small sets because the price of the product is high during the planting season. Tomato growers may tend to extract seeds from off-type fruits that cannot be sold in the market. When the size of the dry set and the fruit shape are genetically determined, farmers are definitely selecting in the wrong direction.

Other seed qualities are often poorly taken care of. Poor storage conditions resulting in low seed purity and germination can hinder crop production especially in non-traditional crops (e.g. maize in lowland tropical areas), despite sometimes astonishing local methods. Very limited knowledge of (seed transmitted) diseases can lead to accumulation of pathogens. A common practice in vegetable bean production is the use of the last pods of a crop to extract seeds. This increases the danger of transmission of diseases that have accumulated in the crop during the growing season.

Availability

One of the major advantages of local seed supply is the high level of availability of seed to a wide range of farmers who cannot afford to purchase certified seeds. There are some important limitations however; the most important being the absence of an anti-cyclic production mode and the lack of a back-up system in case of disasters. Local seed supply is generally high after glut-production seasons and low grain prices, and is generally low in cases of hunger when grain prices are high, especially in crops where the plant parts used for seed can also be consumed, such as cereals and legumes.

The formal seed sector can spread such risks by producing seed in different regions and by offering a premium seed price to growers. In local seed supply systems, acute seed shortages are likely to happen more often. Natural and man-made disasters such as civil strife can very seriously disrupt local seed supply both with regard to quantity and (genetic) quality. When large numbers of people are displaced or when cultivation is impossible for more than one season, seed supply can be seriously disrupted. When large areas are affected the sheer survival of the irreplaceable adapted land-races is at risk in conjunction with the disappearance of social structures and their local knowledge systems.

Formal seed systems, although valuable to supply seeds of a number of crops to certain groups of farmers in developing countries, are unable to reach large numbers of farmers. Their lack of sustainability mainly derives from economic parameters. Local seed systems, which prove very valuable to supply large quantities of seed, appear to neglect some quality aspects. Despite their long time existence, their effectiveness and eventually sustainability may be threatened by rapid changes in the agro-ecological or socio-economical conditions.

Integration of both systems may yield the most effective and most sustainable way to secure the supply of optimum quality seeds of all crops to all farmers. Integration can mean the improvement of either the formal or local system by introducing some positive aspects of the other. In cases where physiological seed quality is a problem, improved seed harvesting and storage methodologies may be introduced while leaving all other aspects of seed supply intact.

Where physical seed quality is a major problem, the use of small scale seed cleaners may be promoted. Where genetic quality of seeds is a bottleneck, new varieties may be introduced into the local experimentation and diffusion system. Various models for accelerated variety diffusion exist, such as random distribution of samples, directed distribution of production kits, sale of samples and different levels of on-farm demonstrations and on-farm research.

Where suitable varieties cannot be bred by conventional methods, adapted breeding strategies can be developed to enhance selection efficiency by adapting the selection environment or the selection procedure. Where availability of seeds is the major problem—in cases where this is not related to any of the above—seed security centres may be established. Cromwell et al describe some experiences with such centres.

Another approach is to promote seed production by farmer cooperatives in a semi-formal manner, as described by Garay et al. This is done by directed subsidies or tax relief for starting seed enterprises and temporary relaxation of certification standards. The possible solutions to specific problems may require a number of activities, ranging from surveys, priority analysis, technology development and diffusion of technologies, which have been described by Tripp and Woolley for on-farm research.

Since there is evidence that in many cases women are responsible for seed selection and storage a strong gender aspect has to be included. The site and crop specific analysis of the strengths and weaknesses of existing seed supply makes blueprint methodologies and blanket recommendations, such as used in the formal sector, irrelevant. For most quality problems, basic technologies already exist. They may have to be adapted to local conditions only.

For variety development for the remote and resource-poor farmer on the other hand, methodologies are still to be evaluated. This means that in most cases the importance of surveys, farmer participation in local adaptation of technologies and diffusion of technologies have to be stressed. This requires an important input of the social sciences in seed supply development. The variety of possible technical improvements corresponds with a wide range of possible ways to transfer knowledge and/or materials to farmers (and vice-versa).

General extension messages can be used to improve, for example, storage methods. Another option is to train selected farmers on improved seed production. They could either transfer the technology to other farmers or they could become specialised (local) seed producers. These farmers could also be a suitable alley for variety introduction, especially when they are the same persons who are involved in on-farm research.

Farmers' Knowledge and Practices in Smallholder Seed Production

As part of their overall fanning system, farmers have developed seed supply systems for maintening and developing seeds and planting materials. These systems have been called 'traditional', 'local' or 'informal' systems, as they are often seen as opposite to 'modern' or 'formal' seed supply systems. Although totaly 'informal' and totally 'formal' seed supply systems do exist, in most cases seed supply systems contain elements of both. In most developing countries, especially in marginal areas and areas with variable ecological conditions, seed supply systems contain more elements of the 'informal'.

In 'modern' agriculture 'formal' seed supply systems are dominant. The importance of farmer-managed seed production systems has been largely underestimated by breeders and seed technologists. Consequently these systems have not received sufficient research attention. Information on the subject is scarce and is more likely to be found in anthropological and sociographic literature. However, interest in these systems is growing, partly because the high expectations of 'improved' varieties and 'modern' technology have not been realised.

Development of Variety Seeds

There are several indications that farmers' communities

have some capable breeder/selectors, often women, who are involved in a more or less permanent process of selection. They select varieties which are best fitted to the specific agro-ecological conditions of their different fields and to the socio-economic conditions of their farm. In an attempt to cover possible seasonal hazards (drought, excess water, infestations of pests and diseases, etc.) they also plant different varieties within a mixture.

In order to cover many situations, a large number of varieties is needed. For this reason, farmers permanently try out and incorporate new plant material into their production system. This means that newly introduced varieties, even from the formal sector, may become 'local' after some time, particularly in the case of cross pollinating crops.

Farmers usually farmers judge a variety according to their own criteria. Although yield is always important, small farmers tend to prefer yield stability to maximum yield, in line with their policy of risk avoidance. Apart from selection criteria like resistance to pest and diseases, which are generaly important, other specific criteria may be included, such as growth period, suitability to intercropping, taste, shape, colour, secondary uses, etc. To ensure that important criteria are not overlooked, farmers' judgements must be incorporated into any outside selection work.

Seed Production, Storage and Diffusion

In retaining seed for the next season, most farmers apply some selection. However, the intensity of the selection appears to vary greatly. Seed can be selected before or after harvest, and is sometimes produced in plots which get special treatment. Farmers have developed a variety of storage practices, such as in the smoke of the kitchen, in ashes, in sealed containers or in calabashes. Observations also indicate that the non-genetic quality of farmers' seed is often as good as seed from the formal sector. There are a number of systems for diffusion of introduced or locally developed varieties based on traditional social networks.

3

Approaches to Seed Marketing

Governments in developing countries have succeeded in establishing seed legislation as well as seed production and trading activities, government supply objectives are frequently not met and seed stocks remain unsold. This may be because the public sector usually operates passive distribution systems, simply stocking outlets from which the farmer can collect seed but often leaving many outlets unstocked or with the wrong varieties. Such systems are not responsive to the needs of the farmer.

However, by introducing a commercial perspective and applying sound management and marketing techniques these passive systems can be transformed into active marketing systems which may prove far more beneficial to the farmer and the supplier The principle that marketing is about identifying anticipating and satisfying the needs of the farmer, as well as realising the objectives of the supplier, is fundamental. Even if public sector objectives are not necessarily profit oriented there is no reason why a public organisation should not adopt sound management and marketing techniques.

Seeds arc particularly important in farming systems where resources are scarce since a significant contribution to productivity can often be gained solely from the seed used, independent of other purchased inputs. Thus, the genetic potential of seed largely dictates crop yields and the productivity of other agricultural inputs and cultural practices.

The situation in countries where the seed market is immature is that improved plant varieties are released to farmers mainly through public sector research. In markets which support a mature seed industry, private sector companies are usually the main source of new varieties, with the public sector concentrating on basic breeding and releasing new genetic material rather than finished varieties ready for commercial use.

The degree of public sector involvement in the release of finished varieties reflects both government policy and the extent to which the private sector has developed. While governments may support national breeding programmes, in order to ensure a flow of improved varieties of the major crops, investment by the private sector is also to be encouraged. The private sector is only likely to become involved if a well-regulated market exists and the products of private research are granted protection through Plant Breeders' Rights. This is particularly necessary for inbred crops.

Hybrids, and many vegetable crops, have a degree of in built protection as the breeder controls the parent lines. Initially, therefore, private companies will probably begin supplying the seed of the more easily controlled and more profitable hybrid and vegetable crops, leaving the public sector to concentrate on the more strategic, higher volume, non-hybrid crops.

Seed Policy

The role of governments should be to create a legislative framework which supports national seed institutions, creates the appropriate economic environment and minimises government interference in the market. In such circumstances the private sector may be encouraged to play a greater role while guaranteeing the availability of seed of reliable quality to the farmer. Over the past ten years many developing countries have initiated structural adjustment programmes in order to correct severe domestic economic problems.

An important part of these programmes consists of reducing the role of the state in economic activity. One specifi : area where changes are occurring is in the marketing of agricultural inputs and produce. The pressure for market liberalisation is based on the belief that economic performance will be enhanced by involving the private sector and creating competition. However, private business may not always be able to fill the gap left by departing state enterprises. As a result, it may be necessary to combine professionally managed public operations and private enterprise.

In privatising state seed organisations, for example, there is an added risk that private monopolies are created in the place of state monopolies. A steadily increasing number of countries is embracing privatisation and seed market liberalisation as a solution to the under performance of public sector seed supply. But no practical improvement in seed supply will result simply by declaring such a policy. Any such change has to be accompanied by a significant shift in attitude and a willingness to implement change.

Seed policy should also create a positive economic environment by:

- removing the barriers to seed trading;
- liberalising investment and ownership regulations;

- adopting a public sector pricing policy which supports the concept of fair and equal competition;
- supporting agricultural services and promoting the use of inputs, including seeds, through the extension service;
- providing adequate funding to government seed institutions involved in the administration of seed legislation;
- making full use of public sector seed facilities.

Varieties of seeds distributed through the public sector are usually under the control of state-run organisations although, where private seed companies are established, they usually have access to these public varieties. Seed distribution may be undertaken by public sector agencies, cooperatives or the private sector or, as is often the case, by more than one of these channels at the same time.

Direct government involvement on a commercial scale tends to restrict the opportunities for private enterprise. The public sector usually works in such a way as to limit a developing private sector from competing on equal terms through a number of practices, some of which are listed below:

- capital investments are provided by government and donor agencies without the requirement for repayment of loans;
- organisational overheads and working capital charges are not included in seed pricing considerations and any trading losses are written off;
- costs directly attributable to the seed activity are spread through other divisions and thus may not be reflected in the price of seed;

– high volume cereal seed is priced at low levels in an attempt to encourage seed use.

It is desirable that there should be a parallel development of both the public and private sectors in the formation of a national seed industry. If well planned and managed the best interests of farmers will be served and government objectives realised. India is a good example of this parallel development although private business has voiced some concern over the use of subsidies which distort the market.

Seed Production and Distribution Organisations

Ministries are normally given the responsibility for seed production and distribution programmes in those countries in which the state is directly involved in the supply of agricultural inputs and where there are no other reliable and effective channels. The mandate of government departments is usually to serve all categories of seed user. Therefore, they are obliged to supply a diverse range, including seeds of low value grains, to areas of both high and low productivity. Being, in general, non-commercial in nature, government departments tend to be heavily bureaucratic with time consuming communications processes which are not responsive to the needs of the market.

Public sector corporations have an independent management and financial structure, albeit underwritten by government. As such they may have some financial autonomy but their operational strategies and approach to pricing are usually determined by official policy rather than by market forces. Management is frequently expected to operate amid conflicting social and commercial objectives, while not losing money.

Although profit may not be an actual aim, pricing to achieve full cost recovery should be. State-owned seed corporations may be integrated plant breeding, production and marketing organisations or simply act as the seed supplier with breeding being part of government-financed research. Distribution may take place through government supply points, direct from seed plants or through private dealers. If a seed corporation is well managed, embracing commercial principles, then the option exists to attract a private sector partner in a joint venture.

In the seed sector private enterprise involvement can range from international seed companies and national seed businesses to local suppliers working in perhaps just one region of a country. Private businesses should operate within the framework of government seed legislation thus giving the farmer consumer protection. The distribution of seeds takes place through retail outlets which can receive their supplies directly from the seed producer, through intermediate distributors, or through wholly integrated companies which control all the major functions of breeding, production and distribution and have a complete sales network.

Such companies will concentrate their activities in those market segments where there is commercial demand and on those crops which can be marketed profitably, for example, hybrids, vegetables and seeds which are not retained by farmers for replanting.

The main function of a cooperative is to act on behalf of its member farmers in providing them with inputs and in the marketing of their crops. Individual cooperatives can be members of a single centralised state organisation or independent, if owned directly by the farmers themselves. Cooperative groups are well placed to become involved in seed production on an independent or contract basis and can act very effectively as marketing agents. A good example of an independent cooperative is the Seed Coop of Zimbabwe, the success of which depends on the mutual cooperation between government and the mainly privately owned seed cooperative. The Co-op sells seed at prices which are agreed with government and surplus funds are distributed to members.

Yet another kind of organisation is one in which individual seed producers come together to form an association. In the beginning, an association produces improved seed from those crops which are planted by farmers in its immediate vicinity. As the association gains experience and seeks the services of technically competent personnel it may extend the scope of its activities by adding new crops and seeking new markets.

4

Understanding the Market

Market Research

Market research is just as important for a small seed company as it is for a large national organisation. If a small seed company does not have the resources to support one individual to carry out market research, it still needs to devote time and resources for such information to be gathered. It is obvious that the better the quality of the marketing information the better the quality of the decisions that will be taken. However, there are costs involved in gathering and analysing information, and it is therefore necessary to identify and focus on the most important issues.

Seed companies must decide the information that is really needed and set priorities accordingly. The kind of information that is needed involves finding out not only how large the market is, but also what factors influence farmers in their buying of seeds and the particular varieties they choose. Such information is categorised into:

- quantitative data which is factual and considers how big a market is in terms of volume and value, what percentage of farmers buy seed and what share a given variety has. This helps in planning seed production and market development activities;

- qualitative data which is about attitudes and opinions, such as why farmers buy seed and how they select a variety. This helps in variety research programmes, seed production planning and in marketing.

Marketing Information

The information required to make business decisions and to plan and control seed marketing activities falls under the broad headings of:

- general economic and political factors;
- the market place;
- the company and its products;
- the competition;
- the distributors;
- the farmers;
- the traders and industrial users who buy farm produce.

Considering the above headings, the following items are not intended to be an exhaustive list, but a guide to the kind of information required by managers of a seed company and how it might be used. The information required on general economic and political factors includes:

- national economic performance and political indicators;
- agricultural policy;
- seed sector policy;

- seed legislation;
- infrastructure development;
- crop and regional development assistance;
- industrial development in the food sector.

These are factors which should be considered in longer range planning and when making investment decisions. They are important when setting up new breeding programmes, as ten years may elapse before the new products become available. The following information is needed about the market place:

- size, volume and value of seed required;
- structure, farm size and type and regional differences;
- trends, changes taking place in the market;
- demand;
- seed supply, the volume of seed certified, imports;
- import regulations and duty payable;
- transport;
- geographic and climatic factors.

Such market data are used when creating sales forecasts and making seed production and purchasing decisions. This basic market data is also needed when consideration is being given to new products and markets.

Information required by managers on their company and its products:

- the image and reputation of the company among distributors and farmers;
- satisfaction of the dealers and their customers with the company's products and service;

- aspects of the company's product presentation and service which should be improved;
- the responsiveness of the organisation to customers' needs and changes in the market;
- the reason why farmers choose the company's products, e.g. for cost benefits, technical benefits, superior yield;
- new products in the pipeline;
- progress reports on production and processing and stock available for distribution.

Several of the above factors fall into the category of qualitative data. This can be collected by questions to customers and may be used in making changes to the internal organisation of the company as well as in planning promotional campaigns. Also included is internal information, such as variety performance and stock availability, which is required by management for day-to-day operations.

Information required about competitor companies includes:

- ownership and organisational details;
- market shares by variety, breeder, distributor;
- new varieties undergoing official trials;
- distribution systems used, number and location of outlets;
- pricing to distributors and farmers, price history, margins and commission, terms of trade;
- promotional activities, extension, product and market support, advertising, packaging;
- number and location of sales representatives and their areas of operation;

- dealers shared with other suppliers and how much they sell from each company;
- responsiveness of competitors to customers' needs and changes in the market.

In a market economy seeds of the same or similar varieties will be available from various sources, allowing customers to choose between different brands. It is therefore important to know as much about the competition as possible since choice is based on many factors, not just product performance. Seed companies will also require the following information on their distributors:

- the company's distributors and their location;
- methods of communication with the distributors;
- their purchasing pattern and history;
- the level of support they need;
- the factors limiting their purchases of the company's products;
- their financial soundness;
- alternative channels of distribution.

This is operational information that is used to manage and control the channels of distribution and to evaluate alternative methods. Information needed regarding farmers includes:

- factors which limit or influence their demand for seeds;
- land ownership and who makes the buying decisions;
- banking and credit sources to which farmers have access;

- agronomic problems such as pests, diseases and weeds;
- the leading farmers in the area;
- literacy level;
- availability of transport and in what form;
- sources of information used by farmers.

Customer information of this type helps in market planning and focusing the target of sales and promotion efforts. Such information is also useful to distributors and dealers. Indeed distributors and dealers may be used to collect information on farmers. Finally, information is required from the buyers of farm produce grown from the company's seeds. This information includes:

- marketing arrangements that exist for farm produce;
- the uses to which the product is put;
- quality requirements;
- quality premiums available to the farmer;
- contract growing systems and whether seeds are supplied or varieties specified;
- developments in the commodity and final products markets, including demand, price and replacement by substitutes.

This will indicate the extent to which the buyer or industrial user influences the farmer's decision to buy a particular seed. Often industrial users provide seed as part of a buy-back contract. Research gives an indication of the strength of the market for farm produce and, therefore, future demand for seed. There are also quality factors which should be understood and incorporated into plant breeding objectives. Examples are barley used for making malt, wheat used for bread making and cotton used for high quality yarn.

Information Sources

Internal Information

Much of the information required by management can be found within the company so that is the best place to start. Often, extensive records are kept but the data is not made available in a form that can be readily used by management. All organisations collect information in the course of their everyday operations. For example, orders are received and delivered, costs are recorded, activity reports are submitted and invoices are sent out. As an example, the information that can be derived from invoices includes:

- sales by territory:
- sales by customer type (if they are classified):
- average order size by customer type and area;
- sales by product type and variety, package type and size;
- average sales by the personnel responsible;
- frequency and seasonality of orders;
- sales incentive or promotion programmes;
- payments outstanding.

Such information helps managers analyse sales performance, target the sales and promotion effort, evaluate distribution channels and dealer performance, and follow up late payments when credit is given.

External Information

There are many sources, depending on the particular type of information required. Some of these sources are:

- dealer network
- variety and types of seed grown, buying habits, competitors' products and prices, stocks
- farmers and farmers' organisations
- consumer profiles, factors affecting seed purchasing, level of input use
- government agricultural and trade statistics
- crop area, yield and farm size and number, imports and exports
- provincial and regional government offices
- precise statistical data and local knowledge, support programmes
- government organisations breeding institutes, certification and extension services
- crop agronomy and variety, information, seed certification tonnages
- international agencies
- statistics, special studies, crop and commodity reports
- seed associations and other trade organisations
- seed company listings and details, seed production and supply data
- product catalogues
- competitor product range, treatments, prices, terms of trade, sales organisation

- trade directories
- company listings, product details
- related industries
- agrochemical, fertiliser and machinery companies
- agricultural banks
- economic data, credit and loan facilities, linkage with development programmes
- universities and other teaching establishments
- library facilities, technical and research data, studies and specialist knowledge
- journals and publications
- technical articles and special features, product and market reviews

Attention must be given to the accuracy and reliability of the source and attempts made to cross-reference and double check. Data must be treated with care. Seed import, export and production figures, for example, may no/distinguish between seed used for sowing and oil seed for crushing.

There will be occasions when it is desirable to commission work from professional market research organisations. In order to get exactly the right kind of information from a commissioned study, it is important to adequately brief and agree on Terms of Reference with the company selected to carry out the research. This involves defining with care exactly the sort of information that is required.

If the research is conducted by means of a questionnaire, the market research company will begin by preparing the questionnaire and running a set of pilot interviews. The company should then report back to the client before undertaking the survey proper to ensure that the questions have been formulated appropriately, and make any necessary recommendations.

Although commissioned market research is expensive and will be beyond the means of many small seed companies, serious consideration should, nevertheless, be given to seeking professional help when the consequences of making business decisions based on insufficient or inaccurate data can be costly.

Information Gathering

The main techniques for gathering data are through:

- desk research;
- personal interviews;
- group discussions;
- telephone interviews;
- postal surveys.

Desk research is the term given to making use of data that already exists or published data which can be accessed. This is always the starting point of any market research project but the information may not provide sufficient detail or may be out of date, thus making it necessary to undertake field research to generate new information. Government statistics provide information on a regional basis such as crop areas, yield, number and size of holdings. These can be used to determine total seed demand and give information about the farmers and the quantity of seed they will be likely to use.

Fertiliser distributors will have records which will indicate the general level of inputs used. The seed certification service will know the quantity of seed that has been certified and the extension service will be familiar with the use of the different categories of seed, e.g. seed retained on farm, unlabelled and certified seed. Information needs to be collected in such a way that the respondent has little opportunity for an opinion to tee expressed. For example, questions might be phrased as follows, "What variety of rice did you grow last year?"- "What area did you plant?"

Conversely, qualitative information may require a more discursive approach so that farmers are given the, opportunity to express their opinions with questions like, "Variety A, B and C are similar. " - "Why did you choose variety B.?" Thus, the researcher needs to consider the type and quantity of information required in choosing the method of communication.

Face-to-face interviewing is the best form of contact as it involves two-way communication, providing instant response and reaction. The information is usually immediate and the closer personal approach is frequently a good way of getting detailed and accurate information. However the process can be time consuming and expensive if travel is involved. This form of contact and information gathering happens all the time on an informal level, but for a formal study it requires a very structured approach and the use of a questionnaire.

Group discussions bring a group of people together to judge their opinions and can be used to test new ideas and concepts. But the presence of a professional is needed to ensure that the exercise is effective. Questionnaires are often used as a way of collecting both quantitative and qualitative information through face-to-face interviews, by post or over the telephone. Some principles of questionnaire design are:

– the questionnaire must suit the contact method to be used;

- questions should be unambiguous and unbiased;
- questions should be asked one at a time;
- questions should be clearly related to the objectives of the study.

Questions are of three basic types:

1. Single choice, yes/no, for example,

   "Do you buy rice seed ? "

2. Multiple choice, for example,

   "How often do you buy rice seed ? "-"Every year?...

   ... Every second, third, fourth year?"

3. Open-ended, for example,

   "Why do you not buy seed each year?"

Using these three types of questions the questionnaire can be:

- structured using all single- or multiple-choice questions;
- semi-structured using a combination of the above with open-ended questions;
- unstructured using open-ended questions determined by the interviewer.

As a guide, for large samples using a team of interviewers looking for relatively simple information a structured or semi-structured questionnaire should be used. An unstructured or semi-structured questionnaire would normally be used for in-depth interviews of a smaller sample group.

Market Segmentation

Individual customers have different needs but an

organisation cannot provide a different product and service for each customer, neither can customers be served properly if they are all treated as being the same. The technique of market segmentation is used to help solve this dilemma. Market segmentation is the process of identifying and then separating a total market into parts so that different marketing strategies can be used for each part. This involves collecting marketing information about the different segments that the company has identified.

Distinguishing between the different characteristics and needs of consumers order to identify a particular market segment is called differentiation To be of value to the marketing manager the segments should include, within the segment, customers that are very similar to each other but, between segments, customers that are as different as possible from each other. The manager will look for segments that are large enough and have sufficient purchasing power to give an adequate return and make a differentiated marketing approach worthwhile. This information is critical to the selection of target markets. An example of differentiation could be the difference between vegetable growers with small holdings supplying a range of fresh produce to local markets and specialist growers producing vegetables to supply a canning factory.

Segments on the basis of geographical factors include:

- location
- physical characteristics, rainfall, soil types, altitude
- irrigated or dry land
- different cropping patterns and input regimes, farming systems

Segments on the basis of crop species can include:

- type or variety
- white or yellow maize, hard or soft wheat
- season
- winter, spring or summer sown
- maturity groups
- early, medium, late
- use and quality
- forage or grain, feed or bread making, oil or meal, etc.
- non hybrid or hybrid vegetables,
- maize, sunflower

There are a number of broad classes of crops. These include cereals, pulses, oils, fibres, industrial crops, vegetables and flowers. Vegetables can be further sub-divided by type, e.g. leafy, legumes, fruit, and root. Each of these types has, in turn, a range of species and varieties. Thus a complete study could involve too much work for the resources available. Crops must therefore be chosen which are directly relevant to the company's business or form part of an evaluation of new opportunities.

Farmers can be grouped according to the kind of farm they operate; since different farms have differing needs the services provided to each type will require specialists who can meet the requirements of that particular farm type. Accordingly, the marketing manager may choose to separate the larger managed farms for personal attention and target farmers who sell their crops for cash rather than those who retain crops for use on the farm.

5

Advertising and Promotion

Resources invested in variety development and seed production will be wasted if farmers are not persuaded to use the improved varieties. All promotional activities involve sending messages to the distributors and consumers in order to inform them about a company's products and help them to make their decision to buy a particular variety or brand of seed.

It is important to monitor how effective this communication is by ensuring feedback from both the dealers and the consumers. Such communication can be divided into two distinct types:

Non-controllable methods: These are personal recommendations that reflect the consumers' overall perception of the product and service. They are powerful messages and will influence buying decisions. Therefore, it is important to know what farmers think of a product, especially those leading farmers who are targeted in extension work, as their influence may be considerable.

Controllable methods: These are the marketing messages which are carefully designed and directed to achieve the objectives of an organisation's promotional campaign. Types of marketing messages are:

- advertisements
- messages sent via the media to inform and influence the farmer
- sales promotions
- specific techniques designed to increase sales of particular seeds
- personal selling
- the importance of salesmanship
- publicity and public relations
- generalised communication which is designed to promote the company's image rather than that of specific seeds
- extension
- taking the promotional activity out into the held

Farmers in developing countries have certain characteristics:

- they have low purchasing power coupled with a low rate of return from farming;
- they are generally conservative and therefore are slow to adopt new products;
- they may not be well informed;
- they often lack mobility and the means to transport goods.

It should also be recognised that educational and literacy standards will not always be high in rural communities. The use of visual material will help to overcome some communication problems. In all forms of communication, companies should always try to make the subject of seeds interesting and relevant to the consumer. The communication and promotion process must be carefully thought out and the person responsible must be very clear about the aims and objectives and anticipated effect.

A master plan should be created with separate plans for each activity and sales region. These should all be timed for maximum effect and designed to reinforce each other. When introducing a new variety, expenditure will be higher as awareness must be created. As timing is very important a calendar of key events should be drawn up indicating the involvement of all those working on the campaign.

Individual responsibilities must be clearly defined and activities involving other services, such as extension, well coordinated. It is important that the effort is targeted and a good reporting system set up to allow for adjustments to be made during the season and resources redirected if necessary. There is, for example, no point in continuing to promote a product if no seed is available.

Advertising

A company may use an advertising agency in order to benefit from its specialist skills. The assistance provided by an advertising agency may range from the production of a simple poster to a whole series of events and activities linked to a product campaign. There will usually be one person who acts as a focal point with the advertising agency and who would ideally become familiar with the client's business and market.

The process is similar to that described for commissioning market research. Decide what is to be achieved and why, then create a brief which will form the basis of discussion with the agency. The agency can then respond with ideas and costings which will enable a choice to be made. Printed or broadcast media can be used for advertising. It is important to select the most appropriate.

Print Media

This includes newspapers, periodicals, magazines, trade and professional journals. There may be both advantages and disadvantages when advertising in this manner. Some advantages of the printed media are that:

- good coverage can be obtained and, by using the local press and specialist papers, accurate targeting can also be achieved;
- it is relatively cheap and immediate;
- complex messages can be given in print; these last and can be read again and again;
- reply and cut-out coupons with an exchange value can be used to encourage farmers to request further information and buy the product.

Some disadvantages of the printed media are:

- the text, and therefore the message, may not be well understood due to language and literacy problems;
- only limited space may be available;
- printed text has limited impact and colour does not always reproduce well in newspapers;
- a daily paper has a limited life and the advertisements will have to compete for attention with stories and other information.

As well as placing advertisements, press releases can be given to newspapers or features written that carry the name of the company and its products.

The Broadcast Media

This includes television, radio and cinema.

Television: Some advantages of television are:

- the impact will be greater as both sound, colour and movement can be used to convey the message;
- massive coverage can be achieved and some local targeting may be possible.

Some disadvantages of television are:

- it can be very expensive and is only suitable for simple messages;
- the exposure time is short and the advertisement may miss the target audience;
- TV reception may be poor and if local targeting is not possible the message will not be relevant to many viewers;
- there may not be any related interest programmes that will be viewed by the target audience;
- in many countries farmers cannot afford television, although televisions are often available in clubs, bars and other public places.

An interesting example of the use of television is in Zimbabwe where the Seed Co-op positions advertisements prior to the screening of the weather forecasts, which are of obvious interest to farmers. Linked to this is the Co-op's catch phrase "only buy the seed you know" which gives instant recognition when seen and heard in other situations, such as in printed advertising and on packaging.

Radio: Some advantages of radio are:

- good coverage is achieved; this is not confined to the home as people listen to the radio everywhere, including when they are working on the farm;

- it is relatively cheap to broadcast on radio compared to television and advertisements are easier to prepare;
- the incidence of local broadcasting, in local languages, is greater than with television;
- related interest programmes and farming information spots are usually more frequent.

Some disadvantages of radio are:

- reception may be poor in certain areas;
- people don't always listen closely and consequently may have poor recall of the message.

Language problems can be overcome through local broadcasting and there is always the possibility of involving local personalities to add interest and relevance to the area. Radio is useful for making announcements, such as the availability of seed in the area. Another form of broadcasting is the loudspeaker van which can be used to tour villages or towns to make similar announcements, particularly on a market day.

Cinema: In rural locations where cinema is the main entertainment a high proportion of the audience will be involved in farming so this medium could be considered for advertising. Advertising slides are not expensive to prepare and these can be shown during the show.

The outdoor media: Outdoor media include posters, signs and advertising on transport, bus shelters, walls and buildings. These forms of advertising can be used to increase the visibility of the company and its products. Outdoor advertising may have considerable and lasting impact at a low cost if it is well situated and if there is not too much competition for the available space. Exclusive arrangements can always be made for the use of space.

In addition to commercial advertising, retailers should be supplied with signs and crop boards. It is important that good sites are chosen which are highly visible and strategically placed to ensure maximum exposure.

Packaging design. Packaging is a form of advertising. Clear printing, the use of colour, brand or company logo and well reproduced photographs or images are all important components of design.

Sales Promotion

Sales promotion is the term given to describe a variety of techniques designed to encourage customers to buy. They complement advertising and other promotional activities. They are tactical devices that provide incentives to 'buy now', thus sales promotion is short-term (to achieve an immediate effect) whereas advertising is a longer term communications process. The techniques used to achieve these short-term effects can be divided into either selling to the market channel or selling out of the marketing channel.

Selling to the Marketing Channel

These are the techniques which, by providing incentives and support, enhance sales to the trade and encourage the distributors and dealers to stock the product. Some examples follow.

Dealer 'loaders'. These are ways of encouraging dealers to build up their stocks in sufficient time, so that inadequate supplies and last-minute transport problems are avoided. Examples are: offering discounts on orders taken early and progressive, volume discounts on large orders (quantity discounts). These discounts can, of course, be passed on to the customer.

Point-of-sale materials. These are materials supplied by the seed company to the sale points to support sales of their product range. They are used to display and attract attention to the product range as well as to provide information. This form of sales support encourages the dealer to order stocks. Examples of point-of-sale materials include colourful display boxes in which seed packets are placed, particularly vegetable seeds, product information leaflets, seed catalogues and audio-visual displays, such as slides with sound tracks or videos.

Dealer competitions. The larger seed companies can afford to offer significant prizes linked to dealer sales' performance. It is also an established technique in the more developed countries to hold dealer seminars in attractive locations. While it may not be realistic to expect companies in developing economies to incur the high levels of expenditure necessary to organise dealer seminars, some form of incentive scheme may be worth running. Overseas suppliers could also be asked to support such schemes by inviting the 'dealer of the year' to visit the producing country. A dealer will also value the status of seeing his name in print so press releases and dealer names featured in catalogues and advertisements can be used.

Dealer training. Training dealers in the use and benefits of the product is a vital form of support. A dealer will attract customers and sell more if confident and knowledgeable about the product. Training should also cover product care in store and stock rotation as well as retail presentation.

Credit. This again encourages higher stocking and can be used selectively to promote certain product lines. Credit can be used as an incentive to dealers where companies have to compete for shelf space.

Sale or return. This is particularly relevant for the stocking of new products as it provides an element of risk-sharing. However, it can be costly to the supplying company. A return system is used to promote preferential stocking but simply stocking the dealer on a sale or return basis should be avoided as the dealer will have no commitment to sell. Such a system should always provide an incentive to take stock. Thus, for example, returns could apply only to stock taken over and above the previous year's sales. There are, of course, quality considerations and companies may prefer to collect unsold stock for secure storage and relabelling to avoid the possibility of farmers complaining of poor germination in a subsequent year. This can be provided as a service to the dealer with the product remaining the property of the dealer. It is important that the supplying company protects its name and image at all times.

Promotional gifts. Small gifts (give-aways) can be given to dealers as added incentives. The seed company's name can be promoted on pens, cigarette lighters and calendars. These serve the purpose of keeping the company and its brand names in the dealer's mind. Small value items can also be passed on to farmers when they purchase their seed. Larger value items may be given to dealers as presents in return for orders for new products, achieving higher volumes or even for displaying a company's seeds in front of its competitors' products. Many of these techniques may only seem relevant to the more sophisticated and competitive market situations but marketing managers should be aware of the techniques that are used to encourage dealers to stock and to promote one product in preference to another.

Selling out of the Marketing Channel

These are the techniques which assist the retail trade in

promoting and selling products to the final consumer. Some examples follow.

Free samples. Dealers can give out samples of new varieties. The indiscriminate use of free samples can be counterproductive, however, as the farmer may not achieve a good result and blame the variety or may not use the sample as it was free.

Seed exchange. Seed can be exchanged for farmers' grain to overcome initial resistance to buying and using improved seed. This is perhaps more of an extension practice which should be organised by the seed company on a direct basis.

Coupon offers. Refundable coupons can be used offering 'money off' the next purchase to encourage repeat orders or purchases of other products in the company's range.

Price reductions. This will obviously be popular but the danger is that revenue will simply be reduced without significantly increasing sales so the technique needs to be used selectively.

Competitions. Competitions only create interest if they capture the imagination, e.g. a yield competition and membership to a 'yield club' for a certain achievement. They can be organised on a village level or directed at a certain group, such as young farmers.

Premium offers. The offer of an extra product for a promotional price can be made. This could be a joint promotion with a non-seed product or linked to seed of another species that could be grown by the farmer.

Field demonstrations and group discussions. These are both very effective ways of promoting seed products and supporting the local dealer. These topics are dealt with later when seed extension and demonstration are considered.

It is important that, before embarking on promotional activities, the marketing manager is given the necessary support within the supplying organisation as well as among the distributors and dealers. There is obviously no point in starting a promotion without ensuring that sufficient funds and materials are available and that there is the necessary administrative organisation.

Personal Selling

While seed products may be well advertised and promoted, a high degree of personal selling and service will always be required. Seed company staff and, where possible, dealers should always be provided with adequate training and familiarisation with the products they are selling and the market they are selling into. A good presentation of the company and its product range is important in making the sale.

The company should provide the necessary visual material that can be used in both informal one-to-one and more formal group presentations. A ring binder with sequenced seed product leaflets and photographs is a useful way of conducting a one-to-one presentation. A good seed catalogue is also useful, especially for a product group with a large range.

Public Relations

Public relations is defined as 'the means by which a company tries to develop a mutual understanding between itself and its public'. PR is therefore concerned with what people think of both an organisation and its products. The 'public' refers to customers, shareholders, employees, special interest groups, trade unions and the general public. PR is a long-term and ongoing process, its objective being to enhance both reputation and image, thus creating an external environment in which a company can prosper.

It helps convert any negative feelings towards an organisation into positive ones. If favourable attitudes exist, consumers will be much more receptive to the direct marketing activities of the company. It is therefore necessary to identify any unfavourable attitudes among seed dealers and buyers, from which a PR strategy can be developed to reduce the negative effects and build up a more positive perception and image. PR activities include:

- press relations: press conferences and press releases are useful ways of disseminating news items such as stories of achievement, policy changes, management changes and new product launches
- community relations: good publicity can be achieved by an involvement with, and support of, local events and activities such as organising farming competitions and giving awards, e.g. an irrigation pump, to individuals or to a whole village
- editorial activity: the distribution of in-house magazines, annual reports and dealer newsletters with stories as well as product information, brochures, etc., all maintain contact and can be used to target messages to particular groups
- customer care: an extension of the sales contact with dealers or consumer groups beyond the sale; customer care means dealing with any product-related problems, such as poor germination, in order to retain customer loyalty

- sponsorship: this involves supporting local sporting, farming and cultural events chosen not only for their potential exposure but for their relevance to the nature of the business; national farming competitions, for example, can give a company a great deal of exposure through the media
- visits: groups of farmers and dealer scan be invited to the company research station, seed processing facilities and warehouse; appropriate press coverage can be arranged

Seed Extension

Extension is taking the promotional activity out into the field and demonstrating to the farmer the value and benefit of using improved seeds and cultivation techniques. In a competitive market, each company will organise its own field demonstrations to promote its individual varieties and brands.

Field Demonstration

This is potentially a very powerful promotional technique but good planning and execution are needed if it is to have the desired effect. Demonstrations can be used to:

- promote the adoption of certified seed and improved farm management techniques;
- conduct comparative variety yield trials;
- launch a new variety or restimulate interest in existing varieties;
- demonstrate single varieties in a larger block trial;
- teach farmers how to grow crops to maximise variety benefits.

The demonstration must involve proper seed and fertiliser usage, soil and water management practices, weed control and plans protection measures and, if necessary, security measures. In order to plan a demonstration the following are some guidelines that should be observed.

Planning ahead is essential. Points to note include:

- all requirements must be considered, dealers must be supportive, good land and good farmers must be identified a season ahead when any field problems can be seen;
- government agencies, such as the extension services, may be involved so they will need warning of any requests for help;
- resources will need allocating so projected costs will require budgeting, e.g. rent may have to be paid as well as inputs supplied; running field days also costs money;
- to make full use of the demonstration it should be part of an overall campaign so other promotional activities will need to be reviewed.

Great care must be taken in selecting the location. Aspects to be considered are:

- the farmer must have the basic equipment and skills needed for carrying out all the farming operations;
- he/she should be well regarded in the locality and be considered a good farmer; selecting the bigger and better-off farmers can produce a negative reaction;
- the site should be uniform and have no obvious disadvantages which will affect cultivation;

- good access and some space to handle visiting groups is important;
- proximity to passing traffic for maximum visibility of signs should be considered.

In carrying out the demonstration the following steps need to be taken:

- conducting a soil test for mineral deficiencies;
- planning the layout to include own varieties, controls and possibly competing varieties and/or different treatments;
- organising the delivery of inputs and briefing the farmer on the layout and cultivation;
- obtaining sign boards for the perimeter and the individual plots (but these should not be posted until it is sure that there are no unforeseen problems);
- arranging for regular inspection visits and farmer support for subsequent operations;
- planning site use for maximum exposure and advantage at the appropriate stage of development;
- informing all those who will be involved, for example the company, the dealers, the extension service and the media.

During the growing season emphasis needs to be placed on:

- advertising the demonstration and organising visits for groups of dealers and farmers; the dealer should come with his own customers; consideration should be given to who else may benefit from seeing the demonstration and who may influence variety choice;

- monitoring progress, keeping records and taking photographs;
- preparing visual aids and having a supply of product and company literature available;
- thinking ahead to a promotion for the next sales season linked to taking orders during the field day;
- when groups visit demonstration plots, recording names and addresses for future contact.

After harvest, attention needs to be paid to: analysing and presenting any data generated from the demonstration and circulating the information to those who visited and to the host farmer; following-up any prospects with the dealers.

Other extension-related activities could include the company being present at exhibitions, agricultural shows and gatherings where potential customers are present. This can also be part of a PR exercise. Companies should make sure that other organisations such as the Extension Service, breeding stations, agricultural colleges and universities receive samples of the varieties being promoted.

Group Discussions

It is usually not possible to contact enough farmers individually. This makes group discussions a useful way of interacting with them on an informal basis and simultaneously receiving feedback. Such discussions can be organised at a local level prior to the selling season to support the dealer network and should involve representatives from the various sales outlets together with a technical specialist. Visual aids such as video should be used.

Seminars

These are more formal occasions which can be used to disseminate technical information and can involve breeders, sales representatives and extension officers as well as farmers. Seed seminars also provide farmers with the opportunity of discussing their experiences with experts. These occasions can be shared with other related organisations and suppliers, such as chemical companies. This will increase the impact and help to share the cost.

Field Days and Open Days

Field days are usually held at demonstration plots but open days can be held at a research station where plots have been sown. If they are held at the supplier's premises a field day provides an opportunity to show farmers what is involved in putting a bag of seed on a farm and the expenses incurred. Obviously, bringing farmers to a central point can be costly but field days provide an effective PR opportunity and can be used to reward dealers and customers.

Catalogues

Catalogues are an essential sales aid and can range from a simple listing of a limited number of field crop seeds to a glossy colour publication of a large range of horticultural seeds. The catalogue both informs the distributors and consumers about a company's products and services while also helping to convey a company's image. The contents of a catalogue can include:

- the front cover featuring the company name, logo, date, name of product range, cover photograph or art work;
- a listing of contents, if the catalogue is a large one;

- an introduction, highlighting new product additions, company developments, awards, official trial results;
- a map of the sales area covered by the catalogue with the various company locations marked; representatives, seed supply stores and distribution points; names, addresses and telephone numbers should be given where relevant;
- descriptions of terms and symbols used as well as seed quality, grades and treatments offered;
- categorised listing of products by species and variety with appropriate product description, unit quantities supplied, special uses, sowing and harvesting period;
- useful conversion tables, e.g. imperial to metric measurements or local units;
- useful technical information;
- terms and conditions of sale;
- a calendar, possibly featuring the seasonal planting of the company's products;
- a price list, which should not necessarily be an integral part of the catalogue but perhaps an insertion since the catalogue may be current longer than the price list.

A seed catalogue can be expensive to produce which may seriously limit numbers and therefore distribution. Therefore care should be taken to provide a catalogue or brochure which is both economic and serves the intended purpose.

No rule can be given as to how much to spend on promotion but it is one of the easiest ways of spending money and so should be carefully controlled and well targeted. Obviously a judgment has to be made by management in considering how much to spend on promotion but there is a minimum level of activity that must be maintained, as an organisation must be visible to the farmer. At the product level the earning potential of the product will also influence the amount that can be spent on promotion. It is likely that the higher value vegetable varieties and hybrid field crop varieties will be sold in a more competitive market, requiring more promotional support.

At an early stage, a company has to decide on the allocation of funds for promotion. The following are some possible approaches. "What can the company afford?" This is a weak approach as it will not be related to specific objectives and will therefore have no measurable effect.

Allocating a percentage of the sales' value to promotion. This is a more useful approach as it is related to sales and enables a company to match what might be regarded as an industry standard. This can be used as a starting point in costing into the total company budget a sum that can be made available for promotion. The disadvantage is that by adopting this method, a decline in sales in one year may lead to a lower promotional budget in the next, leading in turn to lower sales, and so on.

Individual product targets. This is the most logical approach as it will be related to specific and measurable objectives by product or product group. Obviously priorities will have to be set and choices made within the company budget. A small seed company will not have the resources to become involved in all the activities that have been described but the principles involved are, nevertheless, relevant. A minimum necessary level of product and dealer support can be achieved by prudently choosing the most cost-effective activities.

6

Marketing Plan

Developing an effective marketing plan involves understanding the expectations of the consumer, in order to make decisions about Product, Price, Place and Promotion. Each sub-plan must be prepared to satisfy the expectations of the consumer and to meet the business objectives of the company. The product plan should cover:

- the product range and the number of varieties to be offered;
- the key performance factors, e.g. yield, resistance, grain quality;
- seed specification in terms of quality and treatments;
- new product flow and new variety launch.

The price plan is concerned with:

- pricing policy;
- commissions/margins in the distribution chain;
- dealer discount structure;
- short-term pricing tactics, e.g. new variety, stock clearance.

The place plan needs to consider:

- the distribution networks that will be used;
- intermediate storage and transport arrangements;
- sales territories and responsibilities of the representatives;
- customer convenience .

The promotion plan must take into account:

- packaging type and design, colour, logo and product information;
- the advertising and PR campaign;
- the promotional material and sales aids;
- demonstrations;
- coordination with other organisations.

Marketing Information Plans

In addition to the above, other plans will also have to be made. The marketing information plan is concerned with:

- the internal flow of management information;
- market research projects to be undertaken;
- customer feedback on product, service and promotions;
- competitor review to judge relative marketing performance.

The production plan covers:

- seed production volume targets by variety;
- the quantity and type of packaging that is required;
- the chemicals required for seed treatments;

- the packing schedule and dates that stock is required.

The personnel plan needs to consider:

- the staffing levels required, both permanent and temporary;
- the training that will need to be given to staff and dealers;
- an appraisal system, pay scales and bonus structure;
- line management organisation and responsibilities.

The budget plan needs to cover:

- sales targets and costs of all the associated activities;
- financial objectives, e.g. gross margin, expenses and profit;
- resources required expressed in financial terms;
- performance measurement against budget and controls.

Although the marketing department should have some freedom and flexibility to change tactics, once the marketing plan is approved by management, the marketing department should not change objectives or dramatically alter budgets. Any changes in these critical areas can only be made after consultation with, and approval by, senior management. The marketing plan could therefore be viewed as a contract between management and the marketing department.

Strategic Planning

Managers are frequently too preoccupied with day-to-day operational problems to become involved in longer term thinking. Indeed, businesses can fail due to the failure of management to consider the future. Organisations can be slow to perceive changes. These may be happening to the cropping pattern, with the introduction of competitive varieties, or to the seed distribution system.

The starting point is always reviewing the current strategy. The approach to reviewing that strategy has three main elements which pose the three questions that follow.

1. "What is the outlook for the seed industry and the seed market in the future?" This examines those factors, outside the control of the business, which create future uncertainties, for example:
   a. what if the government relaxed import restrictions on seed?
   b. what if the government removed certain crop subsidies?
   c. what if the world commodity price for a crop fell by half?
2. "How secure is the company's position in the market?" This provides an analysis of the company's position in relation to current and future competition and is an examination of its strengths and weaknesses versus its main competitors, for example:
   a. breeding strength and range of varieties offered for sale;
   b. seed production capacity and cost of production;
   c. location and capacity of storage facilities.
3. "What is the future direction of the company's business and how is this going to be achieved?" In

answering this question a manager is stating the company's broad business objectives and an understanding of how they will be achieved. An example of this might be "to operate a business selling high-value imported vegetable seeds through retail dealers, based on an exclusive agreement with an international seed company, with a view to achieving a five percent share of the vegetable seed market in five years".

However, such a statement can only be formulated once the market situation has been analysed. Also any future plan has to be considered against existing constraints such as finance, staff competence, competition and trading restrictions.

Planning Procedure

Every organisation should have a planning and reporting timetable linked to seasonal activity and the financial year. The activities of the agricultural year may not necessarily coincide with the reporting requirements of the financial year end. As far as possible the planning cycle should fit the seasonal activity of the business.

Planning Techniques

There are several techniques which can be used to assist with planning. They include:

Using charts. A chart gives the opportunity to produce a visual plan showing key events and responsibilities over a twelve-month period. Plans from each sector of the business can be compared and peak workloads anticipated better with critical periods monitored more closely.

Using marketing briefs. These are a series of documents created by the marketing department which help to give both a complete and individual plan for each seed variety. The format should allow for individual sections to be monitored, reviewed and revised, if necessary, thus forming the cornerstone for marketing, sales and production decisions.

Monitoring Performance

Management Information Systems (MIS)

The receipt of an order for a bag of seed initiates a chain reaction which results in that bag of seed reaching the farmer. This not only involves physical action, such as transport, but also administrative action, such as creating a dispatch note, updating stock records, sending out an

The marketing plan forms the basis of monitoring as it details the marketing activities and objectives which can be compared with actual results and progress. Regular updates and forecasts should be made for each reporting period against the budget. This process starts with the salesman who first talks to the dealers and farmers and reassesses the sales potential, then talks to the sales manager who collates the information and updates the forecasts.

Such information helps a manager analyse sales performance, target the sales and promotion effort, evaluate distribution channels and dealer performance and follow up late payments where credit is given. Clearly, no manager can cope with having copies of all invoices sent to him so there needs to be a system, either manual or computer based, which does the analysis and presents a report in a form which can be readily understood. This can be illustrated by imagining a situation that is likely to arise with a company which is distributing seeds throughout several regions.

During the sales season the stock of a particular variety, which has been heavily promoted, has been moved out of the central warehouse to locations around the country. Sales have not been consistent throughout each region with some locations having sold out and not able to satisfy the demand while others are still holding stock. The sowing period is short so it is imperative that the sales manager receives information about the progress of sales in the different regions on a daily basis. Action can then be taken to move stocks between locations and make an additional effort where sales are slow.

The efficient production of reports depends on sound data collection and handling systems. Computers have become an essential tool but the extent to which information systems are computerised will obviously depend on the size and capacity of the seed company. What is important is that any system should be well designed and based on a complete understanding of the real, not assumed or apparent, needs of individual managers. A Management Information System essentially consists of three phases, inputting the data, processing it and producing the output.

Input data can be either internal data or external data:

1. Internal data are stock records, invoices and payroll records.

2. External data are information gathered on competitors. A market survey conducted to evaluate how effective a promotion campaign has been and government agricultural statistics.

Output data is used for planning reports and operational reports:

1. Planning reports are not required on a regular basis. Some form of data handling system will be

needed to produce the highly summarised information as and when required.

2. Operational reports are produced to assist the marketing or sales manager to control the day-to-day sales campaign, e.g. stock reports by product line and location, sales reports by product line and region. Decisions may have to be taken as a result of comparing the actual situation to the plan or budget. Information for such decisions is usually based on internal data and is usually required on a predetermined routine basis, e.g. weekly stock and sales reports.

7

Seed Trade and Seed Supply

Seed Supply in Developing Countries

Seed supply in developing countries relies on two distinct sources:

1. the seed industry, be it public or private, and
2. on-farm seed, which is the main source, particularly in the most remote areas.

Seed Industry

It is difficult to collect data on the commercial seed market in developing countries. However, it is possible to say that the commercial market represents less than 10% of the seed consumption, in particular for the staple food crops. This is due to several factors, but the most important one is certainly the weakness of the seed distribution networks. Due to the lack of involvement of the private sector, the number of seed suppliers is not sufficient. In some countries, seed production and distribution is a public sector monopoly.

On-farm Seed

On-farm seed production is the main source of seed in developing countries, in particular for small-scale farmers

(SSF) in the most remote areas. For some food crops such as sorghum, millet, cowpea, cassava and sweet potato, on-farm seed or planting material represents more than 90% of seeds used by the farmers. It must be noted that this percentage is an average, since figures vary a lot according to climatic conditions: after droughts, farmers have no or little on-farm seed available and, therefore, require access to commercial seed or seed provided through relief operations.

On-farm seed must be considered as a major component of seed supply and seed security in developing countries, but it is not a stable one. Consequently, it is difficult and very risky to develop a sustainable seed security strategy based only on such a component.

Seed Security

Seed security is one of the most important issues in developing countries in particular in countries or areas frequently subject to droughts or other natural or human disasters.

Current Situation

Many countries and international Organisations have already tried to develop seed security strategies at different levels of integration. The different strategies developed up to now are:

1. Conservation by the farmers themselves of small on-farm saved seed stocks for their own needs;
2. Establishment of small seed banks to be managed at village or community level;
3. Establishment of national seed security stocks; and

4. Development of sub-regional or regional seed security networks.

Options 1 and 2 function well in the case of a normal year, but usually fail in the case of disaster. Option 3 aimed at establishing national seed security stocks is a basic strategy in drought-prone countries, but stocks should not exceed 20-25% of the annual seed requirements due to high costs to conserve such stocks. Option 4 aimed at developing seed security networks in order to facilitate co-operation among countries in providing farmers with good quality seeds of suitable improved varieties, is certainly the best solution. Indeed, it seems obvious that achieving seed security at sub-regional or regional level is more efficient and cost-effective than at national or local level.

An indirect objective of seed security schemes is also to limit seed donations as carried out currently by many bilateral or multilateral relief programmes. Indeed, it has to be noted that in the case of emergency supply, farmers are frequently provided with seeds of poor quality (as regards germination or health) or of varieties which are not adapted to their area. In addition, such emergency supply can have adverse effects on the long-term development (i) through introduction of new pests or diseases or of new genotypes which will make crosses with local varieties or landraces and (ii) in disturbing or destroying existing commercial seed distribution networks. A good alternative would be to modify seed relief programmes in order to promote sustainable private seed sector by distributing seed vouchers instead of seeds.

In the future, the role of the seed industry and seed trade to achieve seed security at regional or sub-regional level on a sustainable basis should be increased.

International seed trade, seed production and seed distribution should be mainly the responsibility of the private sector (whether small, medium or large-size companies or co-operatives). Activities of seed development projects, extension services, NGOs, etc. should focus on the development of seed distribution networks based on private retailers and co-operatives, in particular in the most difficult and remote areas. Seed security strategies should be designed at sub-regional, regional or global level, thus involving the seed industry of neighbouring countries. Pursuant to that objective, barriers to international seed trade should be removed.

Obstacles in Seed Trade

Within the different regions or sub-regions, several barriers to seed trade have to be removed, in order to facilitate exchange of commercial seeds among and within the countries and in order to implement a strategy aimed at achieving seed security at sub-regional, regional or global level. The main obstacles are currently:

- *The weakness of the seed distribution networks*: it is certainly one of the weakest component of the seed trade in developing countries if we want that quality seed of improved varieties reach SSF. Political strategies should have as an objective to strengthen seed distribution networks. Where possible and appropriate, projects, NGOs and extension services should teach SSF how to enter the formal seed market and realise substantial benefits in establishing small- or medium-size private companies or co-operatives to be involved in seed distribution. It would surely ensure sustainability when projects end.

- *Variety release procedures*: most developing countries have a list of authorised varieties, with very long, and sometimes subjective, release and registration procedures. This list is frequently limited to a very few varieties developed mainly by the national agricultural research institute or some international agricultural research centres. Many countries do not allow sale of seeds of non-listed varieties, even if better than registered ones. Simplified registration procedures or voluntary registration would facilitate the flow of improved varieties to farmers.
- *Seed certification procedures*: these procedures limit exchange of seeds among countries having different procedures and standards. Two options would facilitate seed trade at sub-regional level:

  (i) to render seed certification voluntary or

  (ii) to harmonise procedures, rules and standards in becoming member of international organisations in charge of harmonisation (e.g. OECD Seed Schemes) or

  (iii) a combination of both.
- *Lack of international seed trade rules*: only few national seed trade associations and seed companies of developing countries are member of FIS and apply FIS rules and usage for seed trade, which are the basis for seed trade at international level.
- *Lack of protection of intellectual property*: many developing countries signed the GATT (General Agreement on Tariffs and Trade) and therefore the TRIPs (Trade-Related Aspects on Intellectual Property Rights) Agreement. According to the TRIPs Agreement, all countries have to develop by

2005 a national legislation regarding protection of new varieties of plants either by patent or by a sui generis system such as the UPOV (International Union for the Protection of New Varieties of Plants) Convention. Nevertheless, up to now, only a very few developing countries are member of UPOV. This is a main obstacle to have access to improved varieties bred abroad.

- *Unreasonable phytosanitary requirements*: companies wish to be allowed to import and export healthy seeds. They recognise the need for clear and scientifically based phytosanitary regulations. Nevertheless, it must be noted that phytosanitary regulations are currently one of the main obstacles to international seed trade. Therefore, there is a need to harmonise regulations among countries, in particular at regional level. The IPPC (International Plant Protection Convention) provides the frame for such an harmonisation in order to avoid unreasonable and unfair trade barriers.

In order to establish a competitive and modern seed industry and achieve seed security in developing countries, the main recommendations are:

1. To strengthen seed distribution networks and promote, where considered possible and appropriate, the establishment of small- or medium-size private companies or co-operatives to be involved in seed production and distribution in remote areas. In that perspective, governments should decrease subsidies provided to the public seed distributors, in order to avoid unfair competition. Otherwise, the same subsidies should be provided to both public and private actors

involved in seed distribution, in particular in the most remote areas.

2. To facilitate international seed trade, in particular through:
   - Simplifying variety registration procedures or making registration voluntary and thus allowing companies to sell seeds of varieties that governments have not tested and approved, or limiting compulsory variety registration to a few major crops; making registration automatic for varieties already registered in an other country of the same region or sub-region; including private sector representatives in variety release committees.
   - Making seed certification voluntary.
   - Adopting appropriate legislation to protect intellectual property. The UPOV Convention, through Plant Breeders Rights, provides a good solution.
   - Avoiding unreasonable and unfair phytosanitary requirements, which are not scientifically based.
   - Harmonising legislation and regulations in line with international rules, schemes or conventions, in order to avoid unfair barriers. Thus countries should become member of ISTA, FIS, OECD, IPPC and UPOV.
   - Establishing national seed trade associations to represent the seed industry at national level and ensure that industry's concerns are adequately addressed by national bodies. Currently, only a few developing countries have a national seed trade association.

- Establishing regional seed trade associations according to the model in the Asia and Pacific region (APSA: Asia and Pacific Seed Association). Such regional associations would contribute to the development of the seed industry and would facilitate regional seed trade. It would also provide a forum for policy discussions and exchange of information within regions.

3. To involve extension services and NGOs in the promotion of commercial seeds of modern varieties and utilisation of appropriate improved agricultural techniques. They should also help farmers to become part of the formal seed sector through the establishment of small- or medium-size seed companies or co-operatives. In the meantime extension services and NGOs should, of course, continue to carry out training programmes addressed to SSF as regards on-farm seed production and conservation, since on-farm seed will remain the main seed source for some basic food crops in remote areas.

Seed Trade in Asia

Intellectual property rights (IPRs) and plant breeding have, historically, had nothing to do with each other. In Asia, and much of the South, patents were never allowed on life forms because of ethics, colonial legacies and the threat that statutory monopolies in the health and food sectors pose to peoples' basic needs. Until recently, industrialised countries also excluded living organisms from intellectual property (IP) regimes.

Unlike manufactured products, biological material was considered the realm of nature and therefore regarded as a "discovery", not an invention. Besides, living organisms reproduce themselves, so the tenets of IP law would need to be bent to suit their characteristics. But with the dawn of the hybrid seed industry and, later, the biotechnology-driven life sciences industry, plant breeding has become big business and those businesses want exclusive rights to their research results.

By the mid-1900s, some industrialised countries began to offer limited forms of plant variety protection (PVP) to breeders of new crop varieties. PVP was constructed as a so-called "alternative" to patenting that would supposedly be attuned to the needs of agriculture. It guaranteed breeders a commercial monopoly on the use of their varieties while leaving loopholes open for farmers and other breeders. Since then, both those loopholes have been tightened up drastically and industry is pressuring governments to provide full scale patent rights on any form of tinkering with the very stuff of life.

Today, with the breeding sector dominated by a few mega-corporations, patents on plants and livestock, and draconian restrictions on farmers, are the norm in most industrialised nations. Asia has followed a different path, but it appears increasingly likely that it will meet the same end.

Green Revolution

In Asia, the foundation for the emergence of IPRs on life was laid by the Green Revolution of the 1960s and 1970s, when a package of credit, chemicals, and, most importantly, high-input responsive semi-dwarf varieties of staple crops such as rice and wheat were introduced on the region's farms. The Green Revolution spread rapidly and far. By the early 1990s, just five of these "super varieties" accounted for 90% of the rice growing area of both peninsular Malaysia and Pakistan, nearly half the ricelands of Thailand and Burma, and around a quarter of the rice area of China and Indonesia. These were the heartlands of tremendous genetic diversity of rice only a few decades ago.

The "super" wheat variety called *Sonalika* has taken over half the wheat growing area in northern India and 70% in Bangladesh and Nepal. Other crops followed a similar trend. Green Revolution varieties now dominate most of India's most important crops, accounting for 65% of the rice area, 94% of wheat, 64% of spiked millet, 61% of great millet, 52% of maize, and 46% of finger millet. The Green Revolution engineered the framework for the private sector's entry into Asia's agricultural sector.

First, it established dependency on external seeds—the basis for a private seed market. As Green Revolution seeds stormed through the rural areas, Asia lost much of its abundant crop diversity. In the Indian state of Andhra Pradesh, one study found that the incursion of the Green Revolution led to a loss of 95% of traditional rice varieties without their collection or documentation. Centuries of farmer innovation were abandoned as the Green Revolution institutions—the International Agricultural Research Centers of the Consultative Group on International Agricultural Research (CGIAR), plus their national counterparts—entrenched themselves as the new "leaders" of agricultural progress.

And even as the early gains of the Green Revolution did not last, most farmers, with limited access to pre-Green Revolution seeds or knowledge, remain dependent today on the off-farm breeding programmes of the CG and national scientists. Not without problems. In the words of one CG scientist, Tom Mew, from the International Rice Research Institute (IRRI) in the

Philippines, the new varieties spawned by the Green Revolution lead to "sharp increases in the use of fertilisers and pesticides [that are] needed to ensure bumper harvests." Which means that farmers planting them need cash or, more accurately, credit.

With the Green Revolution, western capitalism came deep into the countryside and traditional diversity was replaced by large-scale, cash crop farming, supported by a system of banks, pesticide merchants, middlemen, and millers. The seed industry has taken a little longer, but it is now stepping in for its piece of the pay-off. From the Green Revolution, the creation of a private seed industry was an easy step. Still, in the eyes of most corporations, the Asian seed market is vastly under-penetrated.

Asia consumes a third of the world's agricultural seed, nearly 40 million tons a year, but it accounts for less than a quarter of the $32 billion annual commercial seed market, with the bulk of sales currently concentrated in Japan and China. By and large, Asia's seed supply still remains the domain of farmers and the public sector. Farmers in India are responsible for at least 60% of the annual seed supply, while farmers in the Philippines produce 80%. But this situation is fast changing.

The private sector stepped into Asia's seed supply in the 1980s when World Bank and US-supported seed programmes and hybridisation of new crops converged. F1 hybrids give high yields but they lose this advantage the following generation, so farmers have to buy new seed regularly. Hybrids now exist for maize, rice, pigeonpea, millets, sorghum, oilseed rape, sunflower and many vegetable crops. Markets for hybrid seed are starting to swell in many countries as in the Philippines, where the area of yellow corn planted to hybrid varieties surged from 10% in 1991 to over 60% in 1997. The hybrid rice seed market is dramatically opening up across Asia, with Monsanto targeting sales in the range of US$1-2 billion per year.

Hybrids are a crucial piece of the privatisation puzzle, but it is primarily the advent of genetic engineering that is behind the industrial sector's surging interest in the Asian seed market and its demands for intellectual property protection. Industry analysts estimate that biotech will add 50% to the value of seed markets, making previously unprofitable markets, such as rice, profitable. The potential revenue has generated huge mergers between the seed and biotech industries—so much so that the five largest seed conglomerates now control nearly 50 percent of all agbiotech patents. Capturing the value of biotech requires several major changes in the global seed market—key among them, the adoption of broad IP regimes for genetic resources.

Emergence of IPRs

A significant financial attraction of biotech is the opportunity it provides for companies to claim ownership of innovation. Whereas conventional breeding relies on natural modes of reproduction, genetic engineering violates natural processes of reproduction by transferring foreign strands of DNA from one organism to another, even across species barriers. The processes of genetic engineering as well as the genes themselves and the end product, such as a plant variety, are generally regarded as "new constructs" of human intervention and therefore intellectual property.

Seed companies can use various mechanisms to protect such property, including plant variety protection, material transfer agreements, and more frequently, patents. Recently, *The Guardian* of London reported that patents are pending or have been granted on more than 500,000 genes and partial gene sequences in living organisms. Since patents confer commercial monopoly rights, patent owners have power to exert high levels of control over the market. Until recently, patents on living organisms were not recognised. This has begun to change.

On January 1, 1995 the Agreement on Trade-Related Aspects of Intellectual Property Rights (TRIPS) entered into force. TRIPS falls under the World Trade Organisation (WTO) and it obliges all parties to make patents available for any invention, whether product or process, in any field of technology without discrimination by the year 2000 for developing countries and 2006 for least-developed countries. However, TRIPS Article 27.3(b) allows WTO members to exclude "plants and animals other than micro-organisms and essentially biological processes for the production of plants and animals other than biological and microbiological processes," provided that they offer patents or establish "an effective *sui generis* system" of protection for plant varieties. What constitutes "an effective *sui generis* system" is not defined by WTO. This has generated considerable debate—as well as delay in the implementation of TRIPS in developing countries.

Patents and Plant Variety Protection

Patents and plant variety protection (PVP) are two different forms of intellectual property rights. Like any IPR, both patents and PVP provide exclusive monopoly rights over a creation for commercial purposes over a period of time. A patent is a right granted to an inventor to prevent all others from making, using, and/or selling the patented invention for 15-20 years. The criteria for a patent are novelty, inventiveness (non-obviousness), utility, and reproducibility. Although patents were designed for industrial application, with biotechnology, patent offices now grant patents on microorganisms and, in some countries, on all life forms.

PVP gives patent-like rights to plant breeders. What gets protected in this case is the genetic makeup of a specific plant variety. The criteria for protection are different: novelty, distinctness, uniformity, and stability. PVP laws can provide exemptions for breeders, allowing them to use protected varieties for further breeding, and for farmers, allowing them to save seeds from their harvest. In plant breeding, PVP is the weaker sister of patenting mainly because of these exemptions.

In Asia, the seed industry and its allies have aggressively promoted the Union for the Protection of New Varieties of Plants (UPOV) as the appropriate system of *sui generis* protection. UPOV is a small intergovernmental organisation that administers common rules for the recognition and protection of PVP internationally. Most of the 46 UPOV members are industrialised countries, which currently operate the UPOV Convention of 1978 or 1991. Accession to the Union is now confined to the 1991 Act.

Through successive revisions of the Convention, the rights granted to breeders have become more and more similar to those granted under the patent system. While breeders get exclusive commercial control over the reproductive material of their varieties and the right to enforce licenses, farmers planting PVP-protected varieties are prohibited from saving seeds for replanting except under highly restricted conditions. And increasingly in many countries practicing PVP, the right of the breeder extends to the farmers' harvest and the direct products of that harvest.

Asia is now fast conforming to the principles of UPOV. The speed and timing of this process has to do with the need to comply with TRIPS and provide some *sui generis* form of protection over plant varieties in countries that wish to avoid the patent route. But the deeper and more fundamental trend it's part of is the push, from industry, to privatise resources and knowledge within the restructuring of global markets. Numerous Asian countries have taken the *sui generis* option seriously and sought to guarantee their huge farming populations special features to buffer the impact of PVP.

Others try to ensure that some of the royalties captured by industry will flow back into genetic conservation. Thailand, for instance, has created provisions for local communities to secure rights over local varieties, compulsory sharing of profits from PVP-protected seeds and links to biosafety law. Similar thinking has been guiding the drafting process in Bangladesh. However, the overriding trend is *not* toward a world of do-as-you-please *sui generis* systems. It is toward harmonisation. This is what we now see throughout the region. For example, India and the Philippines both started off with somewhat "progressive" PVP drafts, seeking to avoid the worst of UPOV in the implementation of TRIPS.

As those drafts moved further through the legislative pipeline, nearly all those special features were deleted or watered down considerably, to the extent that these countries are about to adopt unmistakably UPOV laws. When and where that process is too slow, direct pressure through bilateral trade negotiations is steering governments to the same end. The trade agreement signed between the US and Viet Nam last year provides that Hanoi will embrace UPOV as soon as possible. So does the Swiss-Vietnamese bilateral IPR agreement. As does the US-Cambodia trade agreement.

Ditto for the latest EU-Bangladesh development cooperation package. Never mind that some of these countries may not have the means of enforcing these laws to begin with. Through a sophisticated mesh of global, (sub)regional and bilateral trade agreements, industrialised countries are working hard to secure the conditions that will provide strategic advantages for their firms. And to penetrate Asia's seed market, that means securing standard UPOV-type laws in all countries—until they wrench the doors open to full-scale industrial patents on life.

Sui Generis in Action

The Asian countries with PVP systems in place so far—and which could therefore be considered TRIPS-compliant—are China, Hong Kong, Japan, Korea, Taiwan and, at least in principle, Thailand. How are they faring in terms of the promised benefits of PVP, such as increased investment, technology transfer and improved food security? It's hard to say, given the short timeframes since implementation and the lack of studies. Japan adopted its law back in 1978 and over 7,000 varieties are now protected in the country.

However, the vast majority are flowers, and foreign companies are securing more rights under the system by the year. In rice, some 600 varieties are protected, but 86% of Japan's rice fields are sown to just 20 of them. Taiwan provides PVP for 62 species, excluding rice. To date, only 22 varieties have been protected—nearly half of which are, again, flowers. Korea set up its PVP system in 1998. Within the first year, 224 applications were filed, a third of them on rice. The public sector is the most active applicant so far there.

In 1999, China joined UPOV as part of its drive to join the WTO. The following year, 66 applications were approved. Just this year, the first foreign companies have secured Chinese PVP—all on roses. Thailand adopted its PVP law in October 1999, but it has not been fully operationalised yet. In the next few years, enormous pressure will be placed on Asian countries to take further steps to complete the legislative processes and tighten the laws in favour of corporate breeders. This is the experience of every single country where PVP has been introduced.

In Australia, the first PVP Act of 1987 contained important concessions to critics of the whole system. A number of these concessions were soon discarded and, in 1994, the Act was overhauled to conform with, and even go beyond, UPOV '91. According to one Australian academic who was involved in the process from the outset, "It may confidently be expected that, if the 1994 Act does not meet the demands of the plant breeding industry, the Act will again be suitably amended irrespective of contemporary declarations to the contrary."

As in all other UPOV member states, the rights for the breeders get stronger and stronger while the "privilege" left for the farmers gets weaker and weaker. The pressure on Asian countries which adopt PVP systems based on UPOV to accede to further demands of global industry will only grow. At the multilateral level, the WTO has yet to define what is meant by an "effective" system of IPR for plant varieties under TRIPS. And in the absence of a full review of this provision, as mandated in the treaty, the decision may be left to WTO's oft-criticised dispute settlement mechanism.

UPOV, which is dedicated to strengthening the rights of corporate breeders, is another actor that will continue to use all its weight to lobby Asian governments to conform to its Convention. As UPOV's former Vice Secretary-General recently put it, "Countries have a great deal of freedom in devising their own laws on genetic resources and farmers' rights and so on, *as long as the new laws do not conflict with UPOV requirements*." In sum, many forces are now converging to ensure uniform intellectual property rights over farm biodiversity in Asia.

PVP on Trial

The few PVP impact studies available suggest that UPOV-type systems do not live up to the promises of their proponents. For example, they do not increase the quality or diversity of plant varieties released by the private sector. In his investigations, Indian researcher Dwijen Rangnekar found no clear correlation between the introduction of PVP and an increased rate of introduction of new plant varieties. He also found that when rates did increase, as with wheat in the UK, it did not lead to increased "inventive activity".

Commercial varieties are genetically quite similar since they are typically based on parental lines provided by public institutions. According to Rangnekar, much of commercial breeding is directed at "cosmetic differences" to serve market strategies, casting serious doubt on the claim that PVP stimulates innovation. A recent study by the International Food Policy Research Institute shows that 30 years of PVP in the US have had no effect on private sector investment in breeding, nor on yields, in wheat—the country's most important food crop.

Although PVP is new to Asia, the Chinese government is already reporting "serious impacts on the free flow of germplasm" from the introduction of PVP such as: breeders not sharing parental lines, reduced use of exotic germplasm in breeding, and lack of attention to *in situ* conservation and farmers' knowledge.

Assault on Seed Markets

For industry, plant variety protection law is the anchor from which it can launch a much more aggressive assault on Asia's seed markets and farmers. Once governments accept and enact PVP, it's a short way further before they open up the patent system to plants and animals. And once that is secured, there is little standing in the way of patents on any form of biodiversity-related material or knowledge. However, this will still take a little time. In the meanwhile, industry has alternatives to enforce its intellectual property goals—and no shortage of apologists who want us to believe that by accepting corporate monopolies on life, the public interest can still come out ahead.

For industry, PVP has some limitations when compared to patenting. And Asian governments are only slowly getting the legislation in place. But, where PVP is ineffective, the private sector already has ways to enforce its own IP protection systems without the IPR laws.

Material Transfer Agreements (MTAs)

An MTA is a contract between two or more parties specifying the conditions under which materials—say, a seed sample—are exchanged. The conditions may cover confidentiality, transfer to third parties, commercialisation, and other issues. MTAs are often used when the materials in question hold commercial value and embody some form of intellectual property that the provider wishes to retain exclusive control over.

According to John Barton and the late Wolfgang Siebeck, legal consultants for the CGIAR, "Failure to perform what is promised [in an MTA] is a breach of contract which gives one party the right to bring action against the other party, such as suing for damages."

Furthermore, some MTAs define the materials, such as gene constructs, as the "technical property" of the provider, "taken to mean, without limitation, tangible property such as... germplasm and the biological materials and derivatives thereof." In this way, an MTA can provide sufficient monopoly control over intellectual *property* in a country that does not provide statutory intellectual property *rights* on plants and animals.

MTAs are thus a *de facto* form of intellectual property protection, governed by contract law, not IP law. However, Barton says that in most countries the obligations of an MTA are not recognised beyond what is permitted under the country's intellectual property law. This is changing in the US, but the relationship between contract law and IP law remains, he says, "at best fuzzy." Nevertheless, according to a 1998 survey, MTAs were used in over 60% of the cases where CGIAR centers—situated in developing countries—got permission to use privately owned technology, mainly from industrialised countries. Significantly, in 30% of the cases the centers could not specify what form of IPR was involved.

Biological Protection

For the seed industry, a crucial form of IP protection can be concocted biologically. Biological IP protection refers here to the development of seeds in which the intellectual property claimed by the breeder collapses or cannot be transmitted through natural reproduction. The most widespread example of biological protection is hybridisation. The yield factor of F1 hybrids deteriorates in subsequent generations, forcing farmers to buy fresh seed from the company every year or two.

However, not all crops can be hybridised in an economically feasible way. With biotechnology, this is changing. Scientists have now uncovered ways to genetically engineer some of these more challenging crops, such as wheat and rice, for cytoplasmic male sterility—one of the most common and efficient ways to produce F1 hybrid seeds. To date, over 60 patents have been awarded worldwide related to hybrid seed production using genetically engineered cytoplasmic male sterility.

Another development in biological protection is Genetic Use Restriction Technology (GURT), more popularly known as "terminator" and "traitor" technologies. GURTs prevent farmers from saving seeds since the genetically engineered plants will not germinate in subsequent generations or will not express a particular trait (such as herbicide resistance) unless sprayed with specific chemicals that activate the right gene.

Industry intends to use these technology protection systems to secure exclusive intellectual property control in the South, where laws and enforcement of IPRs on plants are weak. While several major companies have insisted in public that they will not pursue the technology, a recent report by coalition of groups in Europe identified 60 patents on GURTs—25 of them held by a single seed company, Syngenta—and reported that laboratory and field tests of plants transformed with GURTs have already taken place in the US and UK.

While Asia weighs the pros and the cons of what to do in the complex IP arena, agribusiness multinationals and research labs in the North have already built up an extensive portfolio of patents for genetically engineered plants that are waiting to be transferred to or built upon here. Some of these "inventions" may already be setting foot in Asia as patents on transgenic microorganisms or breeding methods.

The WTO obliges members to provide patents on both microorganisms and microbiological processes. It also requires product-by-process protection, by which any patent on a process automatically extends to the product of that process. A quick search through the online database of the Thai Patent Office reveals over 15 patents on transgenic "microorganisms", most of them covering plants! This should not really come as a surprise, given the environment of IP law today, even if Thailand does not allow for patents on plants.

In the US and Canada, contractual agreements between seed companies and farmers are now standard practice. Monsanto's Roundup Ready® Technology Agreement is the most widely known and enforced example. According to the Agreement:

- The farmer cannot save seed or any other part of the crop grown from the Monsanto seed for replanting.
- The farmer is prohibited from supplying seed to any other person.
- The farmer must pay 120 times the technology fee plus the legal fees if s/he is caught violating the agreement.
- The farmer must cooperate fully with Monsanto's inspections of his/her fields.

While the main purpose of these contracts is to restrict the traditional practice of farmer seed saving and sharing, they are also explicitly designed to curtail research and breeding—which society might call innovation but companies construe as unfair competition. Monsanto's contract for 2001 carries added obligations that place the burden of liability on the farmer and impose binding arbitration as the sole method of settling any disputes, with the arbitration handled by a private company selected by Monsanto.

The seed industry takes these contracts seriously and polices them without remorse. Monsanto has used private security agents and toll-free "snitch" lines to enforce the agreements. In Canada in 1997, seed companies formed a Plant Technology Alliance to "allow companies to enforce their technology position." Within a few months it resulted in 24 out-of-court settlements worth more than $170,000. According to one Canadian farmer now in a court case with Monsanto, "Farmers here are calling it a reign of terror. Everyone's looking at each other and asking, 'Did my neighbour say something?'" By February 1999, Monsanto had launched an unbelievable 525 cases against farmers.

Winning social acceptance of IPR on life is intrinsically connected with winning social acceptance of biotechnology as the path to better food and farming in Asia. Biotechnologists are trying to appease an increasingly critical public with "free deals" on otherwise patented technologies. Their message is: "No IPR, no biotech. No biotech, no progress. But we can cut deals with patent holders to ensure that the poor can access the technology." Very astutely, they are using IPR as a public relations (PR) tool.

Golden Rice

In January 2000, after ten years of research and millions of dollars in public funding, European scientists Ingo

Potrykus and Peter Beyer announced that they had successfully developed a transgenic beta-carotene enhanced rice. This so-called "golden rice" was immediately hailed as proof that biotech will help the poor. But such lofty ambitions were quickly thrown into doubt when the International Service for the Acquisition of Agri-biotech Applications (ISAAA), which conducted a study for the Rockefeller Foundation and IRRI, revealed that there were some 70 patents potentially tying up the technology.

Fearing the complexity and expense of patent negotiations, the researchers quickly signed the publicly-funded technology away to AstraZeneca (now Syngenta), one of the world's largest agrochemical and biotech corporations. RAFI pointed out that the researchers' fears were not justifiable. Of the 60 countries with Vitamin A deficiency—which golden rice is supposed to address—only 25 could possibly honor any of the patents involved. And in these countries, only 11 of the patents could constrain the project locally. Seven of those are held by four transnational corporations (Syngenta, Aventis, Monsanto, and DuPont), two of which have expressed their interest to make the technology freely available to the poor.

The other patents are held by public institutions. Furthermore, ISAAA's study looked at patent *applications* filed through the World Intellectual Property Office, without confirming whether the patents were actually granted or not in the different countries. ISAAA's interpretation of the MTAs involved is also questionable. According to the study, there are around 16 MTAs involved in the development of golden rice.

In ISAAA's view, these MTAs should not be ignored since, while not limiting in any way the IP claims involved, they bind the parties to contract law which is "more uniformly acknowledged and enforced around the world, even in countries which do not have enforceable IP laws." This is an extreme interpretation of contract law that may not hold water. As stressed by John Barton, "Any real barriers are barriers from patents."

Rather than fight a winnable battle against the corporations, Potrykus and Beyer "cried wolf" and allowed the IP hegemony of the rich to trample over the so-called interests of the poor to access technology. Now the IPR hurdles have simply been passed down the line. IRRI, armed with a $5 million special grant from the US government, has just received the first samples of golden rice at its headquarters in Los Baños, the Philippines, and will now develop breeding lines for national programmes to work with. According to IRRI, "It will be five to eight years before golden rice will reach consumer's plates."

In the meantime, the pressure is on the governments of Asia to put the regulatory framework in place, including IPR laws, to facilitate the local testing and commercialisation of the golden rice. Syngenta may have announced royalty-free licenses, but it also made it clear that it expects to get patent protection on the golden rice technology in developing countries. Despite all the frenzy, there is little reason to believe that small farmers will reap any benefits from golden rice.

Syngenta has only agreed to make golden rice freely available to a segment of farmers—those earning less than $10,000 from it each year—and only if the rice they produce is not exported. Certainly, large farmers and seed companies will not appreciate the subsidised competition. Even IRRI's own IPR advisor says that market segmentation is a "practical problem" in areas "where there are both subsistence and large-scale farmers." So who's going to take care of this "practical problem"? Syngenta? IRRI? The national research institutes? At minimum, it would seem that the whole matter of market segmentation and restrictions on exports will require someone to enforce grower's contracts on golden rice farmers. Where IPR is at stake, nothing comes—truly—for free.

Rice Genome Maps

In April 2000, Monsanto made headlines around the world when it announced that it would share a "working draft" of the rice genome with the International Rice Genome Sequencing Project (IRGSP), a consortium of public institutions working together to complete a map of the rice genome. There was plenty of praise for the company's heroic act of "humanitarian science" and plenty more reason to be suspicious. This was a grand public relations ploy—and much more.

According to lawyers, Monsanto has most likely already filed patents on any sequences that it feels have commercial value. And, besides, Monsanto is not giving away the working draft. It is *sharing* the data with the IRGSP and other public researchers according to conditions set out in an MTA. Under the MTA, institutions accessing the data can only pursue non-commercial research with it and are subject to several obligations regarding any intellectual property temptations:

- The institution must regularly inform Monsanto about its attempts to secure IP.
- Monsanto gets first rights to negotiate a non-exclusive license on the IP.
- Monsanto has the right to use in its own research programme any results obtained by third party researchers.

These conditions place Monsanto in an excellent position to patent or negotiate licenses on genes, once the public researchers identify their functions. Monsanto's decision to make its working draft public is really a tactical move to protect itself from competing companies such as Syngenta—which announced in January 2000 that it had completed a map of the rice genome, four years before the IRGSP expects to finish.

Syngenta has already made it clear that it will restrict access to the genomic map and expects proprietary control over any research carried out with the information. According to Thomas Hargrove, a well known rice journalist, "Dr. Steven Briggs, head of genomics for Syngenta, said the company's data would be like a copyrighted newspaper article—publicly available but not free for people to use as they see fit. And if collaborators make commercial inventions, Syngenta and Myriad 'would expect to share in the benefits.' Briggs also told *The New York Times* that while the companies would not seek to patent the entire genome—the raw sequences in the genetic code—they would try to patent individual valuable genes. And he indicated that Syngenta and Myriad were well on their way to finding many of those."

Seemingly oblivious to this new restriction on public research, the Chair of the CGIAR had only words of praise for Syngenta: "This has the potential to usher in a new era of food security—a world where there is less hunger, healthier and better-nourished people, and reduced poverty, especially in rice-producing areas." IRRI is particularly pleased with Syngenta's token offer to *share* the information with IRRI and with "subsistence farmers", even though it is far from clear what that implies.

Collapse of the Public Sector

Asia's incredible agricultural heritage is a product of centuries of free exchange of seeds and knowledge. Agriculture innovation occurs through a fluid process, circulating and expanding from farmer to farmer. During the 20th century, public institutions began to assert themselves in this process, with highly mixed results. More recently, the private sector has stepped in with a very narrow agenda. Now, IPRs threaten to ruin Asia's highly successful agricultural practices. They give preferential rights to already privileged formal sector breeders and fence off the innovative process—leaving farmers on the outside.

Many in the public sector, particularly within the CG system, are resigned to this shift. Citing decreased funding, they welcome a larger role for the private sector all the while insisting that the public sector serve the small farmers that the private sector will inevitably neglect. If this means conceding to American-style IPR regimes, they reason, so be it. But the real-life problems will soon emerge. To illustrate, a large part of plant breeding at public institutions in Asia now employs molecular techniques.

Molecular markers are used to track the incorporation of interesting traits from one variety to another. The technique, known as marker-assisted selection (MAS), allows breeders to tag genes that they believe are responsible for a desired trait with markers and thereby facilitates efforts to breed these genes into commercial varieties. IRRI has already tagged 35 genes of rice with molecular markers. According to IRRI, "Because of their relative simplicity, easy integration into conventional breeding, and minimal background intellectual property, marker-aided selections are expected to be strong driving forces in crop improvement in the future." But MAS also makes it easier to stake claims to "proprietary" genes and thus extend the reach of IP control over genetic resources immensely.

The private sector is onto this track. On September 30, 1999, Monsanto filed a patent in 81 countries on soybeans with enhanced yield. That patent has already been issued in Australia. It covers any cultivated soybean containing certain genes or segments of DNA from "wild" or "exotic" soybeans identified through MAS. The group of genes, which is only vaguely defined, is said to be responsible for enhanced yield. Not only does the patent claim an important trait in soybean breeding, but it also gives Monsanto monopoly rights on *Glycine soja* (wild soybean), particularly PI407305 from southern China and all its progeny.

Further, the patent extends to any soybean carrying the yield genes. This aggressive intellectual property environment makes it very hard for the public sector to survive. While institutes like IRRI, which perhaps can afford the lawyers, try to draw up means of coping with all these growing threats and barriers, their defences are woefully insufficient. From counter-IPR policies to cosy partnerships with the devil to their own MTAs, they are advancing right into the bottomless pit of privatisation.

Public-private Partnerships

International Potato Center and market segmentation

Several years ago, the International Potato Center (CIP), a CGIAR institute in Peru began negotiations with Plant Genetic Systems (PGS) of Belgium to license its proprietary Bt technology for use in transgenic potatoes. Under the initial agreement, CIP could transfer the technology to any developing country, as long as the Bt potatoes were not sold to developed countries. In the second round of negotiations, PGS insisted on market segmentation, but this time they were unwilling to give CIP freedom-to-operate in important commercial markets in the South, most notably India. Before negotiations could advance, PGS was purchased by AgrEvo.

CIP returned to the table to try and negotiate then with AgrEvo, but once again the talks were interrupted when AgrEvo merged with Rhone-Poulenc to form Aventis. Potato production in Asia is a big business, increasingly dominated by foreign seed companies and food processors. For instance, over the last couple of years, Technico, an Australian potato seed company signed a $60 million multi-year deal with global food giant Pepsi-Frito Lay for production of potato seed in Thailand and China. Technico plants have been established in China and India capable of producing 10 million and 18 million Technituber seeds per year respectively.

PhilRice and Akkadix

Researchers need access to germplasm in order to make the step from genome mapping to functional genomics and gene discovery. The genome map of a variety of rice, for example, provides a reference from which genes of agronomic importance can be identified from a wide range of rice varieties. These genes can then be patented. The CG centers and national institutes are highly regarded in certain circles for the germplasm they hold and the breeding they conduct.

In 1999, the Philippine Rice Research Institute (PhilRice) signed an agreement with Akkadix, an American seed company, to collaborate on the development of targeted traits in rice using Akkadix's Rice-Tag technology. While Akkadix gets to mine the "great rice germplasm" of PhilRice's genebank and take advantage of its rice expertise, PhilRice gets an undisclosed amount of funding and the right to use any commercial developments arising from the deal in the Philippines.

So can Filipino farmers look forward to improved rice varieties from the contribution of their seeds that PhilRice has made on their behalf? Not likely. Akkadix is searching for traits already found in rice varieties of the Philippines. In other words, the Akkadix deal bestows upon the Philippines' prime rice research outfit the right to use its own country's genetic resources on commercial terms that will serve Akkadix.

Xa21 rice

In 1995, Pamela Ronald and the University of California at Davis, where she works, obtained a patent on Xa21, a gene conferring resistance to bacterial blight that she and colleagues cloned from the African rice *Oryza longistaminata*. Much of the research behind UC Davis' patent was carried out by IRRI and Asian national research institutes. Nevertheless, the patent for genetically engineered Xa21 rice lies solely in the hands of UC Davis and the International Laboratory for Tropical Agricultural Research, an American institution with its own patents on the transformation process.

In recognition of the contribution made by Mali, where *O. longistaminata* originates, and public researchers in Asia, Ronald urged UC Davis to set up a Genetic Resources Recognition Fund, which would use royalties from the commercialisation of the technology to support students from developing countries studying at UC

Davis. She also pushed the University to agree to give IRRI full rights to develop cultivars using the cloned Xa21 gene and distribute them freely to developing country research institutes. But the national institutes will have to work out their own agreements with UC Davis if they want to *release* varieties containing the Xa21 gene. Such agreements may not come easy. UC Davis is reportedly in consultation with Pioneer Hi-Bred, a major rice seed company in Asia. Thailand's Rice Research Institute has already decided to drop its Xa21 rice project for fear of infringing upon the UC Davis patent.

ICLARM and tilapia

The forces driving IPR in plant breeding have also impacted research in fish, particularly in the area of aquaculture (fish-farming). The UN Food and Agriculture Organisation estimates that 25% of the world's fish stocks are overexploited or completely depleted and that global demand for fish will be met by a 300% increase in aquaculture by the year 2010. Currently, 91% of global aquaculture occurs in the Asia-Pacific region.

In the years ahead, fish farming will largely depend on the African fish tilapia—otherwise known as the "aquatic chicken" because it is easy and cheap to farm and generally suitable for commercial markets. The value of tilapia imports into the US has surged from under $10 million in 1992 to approximately $90 million in 2000. Asia accounts for over 50% of these exports. Japan is another big importer, with much of its tilapia coming from the Philippines. The booming market has perked the interest of multinational agribusiness in all sectors, including production.

According to one business representative, "What was once an industry of small farmers is rapidly evolving into an aquaculture version of agribusiness; relatively large companies with multinational interests controlling an increasing share of production." But the public sector is not sitting on the sidelines. The International Center for Living Aquatic Resources Management (ICLARM), a CGIAR center, and national research institutions throughout Asia are at the forefront of tilapia breeding efforts.

In 1994, with support from the Asian Development Bank, ICLARM introduced its "New Super Tilapia" and launched a joint project to distribute it throughout Asia with the International Network on Genetics in Aquaculture (INGAR). ICLARM and its INGAR partners are investigating new breeding techniques, such as marker-assisted selection, hybridisation, induced polyploidy, and genetic engineering, for applications with tilapia and other farmed fish. Each step brings them further into the realm of intellectual property.

Breeding holds significant commercial potential for the private sector. INGAR shares its germplasm according to an MTA, which prevents the recipient from seeking IP on the germplasm. Yet, ICLARM's Modadugu Gupta admits that institutions seeking IP on modifications that it makes to the material would "probably not" be covered by the MTA. So far, China is the only country in Asia where an outdoor release of transgenic fish has taken place, but a commercial introduction of transgenic fish may not be far ahead.

The US Food and Drug Administration is currently reviewing an application from A/F Proteins for its AquaAdvantage transgenic salmon. According to the company, the fish is genetically engineered to produce high levels of growth hormone and reaches maturity in half the time of non-transgenic salmon. A/F Proteins says that it has found significant interest in China for salmon and Southeast Asia for tilapia and intends to open an office in Singapore in the near future. The company already says it has global orders for 15 million genetically engineered salmon eggs.

Another US company, Connecticut Aquaculture, is working with researchers at the University of Connecticut to produce and breed fast growing, disease resistant transgenic tilapia. Supposedly, the fish grows at two to six times the rate of non-transgenic tilapia. If these company estimates are true and the transgenic varieties clear biosafety hurdles, they will certainly expand commercial breeding. One casualty of this transformation could be INGAR's IPR policy.

According to ICLARM, "ICLARM's policy on IPR on aquatic genetic resources states that it will not normally seek intellectual property protection on any material in its collection of aquatic resources or on cells, organelles, genes, or molecular constructs isolated therefrom or from ICLARM's own breeding activities... However, with the entry of the private sector in to the arena of genetic improvement of aquaculture species, it remains to be seen whether the free exchange of germplasm will continue or the access will be regulated."

CIMMYT and apomixis

Apomixis is a natural method of asexual reproduction found in some plants that results in offspring that are genetically identical to the mother plant. If hybrid crops were engineered with apomixis, commercial seed producers and farmers could replant the seeds they produce without losing "hybrid vigour". Since apomixis is a double-edged sword for the seed industry—reducing the costs of seed breeding but making it much easier for farmers to save seed—public researchers worry that the industry may try to control the technology.

In what's known as the Bellagio Apomixis Declaration of May 1998, leading researchers in apomixis warned that the concentration of legal rights into a small number of hands will prevent the technology from addressing the needs of resource poor farmers. At present there are at least 14 patents on apomixis technologies. The major patent holders are the USDA, Novartis, and Advanta, which owns patents through its subsidiaries Maxell Hybrids and Agripro Biosciences.

The USDA is setting policy on apomixis through extensive negotiation with the American seed industry. To date it has signed confidentiality agreements with more than 20 companies concerning one of its patents. Another apomixis patent holder is the International Maize and Wheat Improvement Center (CIMMYT). This CGIAR center believes it can best serve its mandate by patenting the technology. The patent, according to CIMMYT, will give it leverage to ensure that the technology is accessible to resource-poor farmers.

In July 1999, CIMMYT negotiated a research partnership with a consortium of interested seed companies, including Pioneer Hi-Bred, Novartis, and Limagrain, and the French Institut de Recherche pour le Développement, another apomixis patent holder. Under the terms of the agreement, the companies receive a global non-exclusive license to the research from the partnership. CIMMYT also receives a global license, but it is confined to research products for "subsistence farmers".

According to CIMMYT's Director-General, Timothy Reeves, the companies were reluctant to finalise a definition of "subsistence farmer" and wanted to leave it "grey" until the agreement was concluded. Reeves says that a definition was agreed upon at the last minute, describing "subsistence farmers" as those with farms where over 50% of the harvest is used on the farm. Not only does the definition not encompass many resource-poor farmers, particularly tenant farmers, but it leaves a key question unresolved: will the onus be on the farmer to prove that the farm is a "subsistence farm" when companies send out their agents to police the countryside?

IPRs and Sustainable Agriculture

Farmers constitute by far the largest sector of seed breeders in every country of Asia. It is they who generate the diversity on which the breeding industry has built its billion-dollar empire. There are nearly 100,000 distinct rice accessions in IRRI's genebank, for example, the bulk of which were developed by farmers. Forty years of UPOV has also resulted in 100,000 new plant varieties—however, this accounts all crops combined, not rice alone, and many of them are genetic analogues of each other. PVP and patents are purely intended to protect a small number of formal sector breeders, particularly the handful of transnational corporations that dominate the commercial market. They are disastrous for farmers.

In a narrow sense they restrict the right of farmers to share, use and save seed from their harvests by extending the breeder's monopoly to the harvest of the farmer's crop. Under UPOV, the breeder has the "power not only over the right to produce or sell, but also... the power to specify how this production or sale should occur." But, more broadly, PVP and patents violate the spirit of farmers' rights and set a precedent for their elimination.

Farmer's rights embody the rights of farmers and farming communities to conserve, develop, use, control, and benefit from not only local biodiversity but also rural peoples' knowledge systems and technologies. These rights, which cannot be protected by IPRs, form the basis of sustainable agriculture and recognise the importance of farmer innovation to global food security and well being. Although some countries may be attempting to include some reference to farmers' rights and sustainable agriculture within PVP legislation, IPR is completely alien to these concepts and there is always pressure under IPR regimes to scale back the rights of farmers in favour of the rights of industry.

PVP in particular reduces the inherent rights of farmers to an exemption—the farmer's "privilege" to save seed—which is extremely vulnerable to international pressure, industry tactics and arbitrary political decision-making. It is not surprising, then, that in all countries where PVP has been adopted, farmers' rights have significantly diminished over time—to the point where farmers find themselves constantly policed by industry operatives for violation of seed companies' higher rights.

Transnational corporations dominate applications for PVP and patents in developing countries. At present, 97% of all patents are held by nationals of industrialised countries and 90% of all technology and product patents are held by global corporations. With their economies of scale and IP leverage, transnational companies can rapidly take control of the seed industry once the IP rules are set in place. This should not be confused with foreign investment and technology transfer.

Studies show that PVP and patents decrease germplasm and information flows and restrict technology transfer to fixed varieties with highly limited legal spaces for further breeding. Furthermore, they marginalise farmers from society's view of innovation while insisting that farmers pay royalties to cover the costs of R&D which they had no say in. Public research, likewise, becomes more oriented to the needs of industry, with national researchers worrying more about their accountability to terms of collaboration set by industry than their responsibilities to farmers.

With PVP and patents, farmers end up paying royalties to access their own germplasm, which is tampered with and repackaged in the North. Certain schemes have been proposed to address this unfair arrangement, but they breach the cultural practices of most farming communities. According to a statement on TRIPS released by a global coalition of indigenous people's organisations, NGOs, and networks: "Knowledge and cultural heritage are collectively and accretionally evolved through generations.

Thus, no single person can claim invention or discovery of medicinal plants, seeds or other living things. The inherent conflict between these two knowledge systems and the manner in which they are protected and used will cause further disintegration of our communal values and practices." The message is clear: supporting innovation in the countryside means enhancing the space in which farmers and formal sector breeders can freely exchange and develop plant varieties and knowledge. IPR regimes do the opposite: giving transnational corporations monopolies on the collective knowledge and germplasm of Asia's farmers.

The typical UPOV criteria for plant variety protection—distinctiveness, uniformity, stability, and novelty—encourage breeding for monoculture production systems and are irrelevant to farmers who do their own breeding to produce genetically diverse seeds. This is extremely dangerous. Chemicals or genetic engineering, which the vast majority of Asian farmers cannot afford, will be used to compensate for the crop vulnerability that can be anticipated from such DUSN-driven breeding.

Essentially, Asian countries are in the midst of choosing between two utterly different models of agricultural R&D: one that is driven by TNCs in the North, and the other that is led by farmers and the public sector. By adopting PVP and/or patent regimes for life forms they are choosing a corporate model of plant breeding and, subsequently, a re-organisation of agriculture according to the interests of Northern seed TNCs, which also happen to be the world's largest pesticide and biotech TNCs. These corporations have vested interests in crop uniformity and vulnerability—not the food security of Asia or the well-being of the region's farmers.

Perspectives of People

Most of the official sector in Asia gives tacit support to IPR. For those in power, it is the only way to access biotechnology from the industrialised countries, which they believe will increase agricultural production. Instead of examining alternatives, they tack on provisions to PVP bills that can only delay the inevitable fall out. In general, farmers, NGOs and other concerned social actors have been marginalised from decision-making and there is a danger that many do not fully recognise the urgency of the situation or understand how IPR relates to other structural problems that they are concerned with.

Nevertheless, as more farmers and those working with them face the issue, there is a growing opposition based on a shared perception of what IPRs are all about.

As articulated by Leopoldo Guilaran, a rice farmer from Visayas, the Philippines, "If seeds are patented, it's like cutting off a farmer's arm since you are removing the farmer's freedom to choose seeds and preserve them."

There is widespread agreement among numerous farmers' organisations, and NGOs and professionals working closely with them, that patents on life forms, including microorganisms, must be prohibited. Several coalitions and groups in Asia are pushing their governments to take a strong position regarding TRIPS. They want a thorough review of the Agreement and a broad public discussion about what IPR policies their countries should implement.

The overall objective is to change TRIPS so that it prohibits patents on life forms and makes no requirement for IPR on plant varieties. The South Asia Network on Food, Ecology and Culture (SANFEC) warns that the *sui generis* option in TRIPS is a trap that will force countries to ultimately implement UPOV-type of PVP. Because what constitutes an "effective" *sui generis* system, they point out, will be "determined by industrialised countries and their corporations, and subject to trade sanctions."

Many groups argue that instead of allowing IPR on plant varieties, Asian countries should urgently establish mechanisms to protect and encourage farmers' rights and community innovation. The Indonesian Network on Farmers' Rights calls for legal frameworks to be adopted to protect "the knowledge and innovation of farming and local communities," "farmers' rights over genetic resources," and "seed exchange and cultivation technologies for sustainable agriculture."

The participants of the "Long March" called upon governments and state agencies to "reorient their policies to emphasise alternative agriculture" and set up legal frameworks that "allow countries to bring cases to court when companies illicitly patent biological resources." Among other demands, SANFEC calls upon governments to "develop and enforce a code of conduct for the regulation of all so-called life-science transnational corporations, with a view to protect the rights, livelihoods and food security of their people," and to "ensure accountability of the public research institutions for the protection of the interests of the poor farmers, and for sustainable agriculture, bio-diversity and the rights of the communities over their knowledge, technology, practice and genetic resources including all plants, plant-forms, and animals."

These positions boil down to a completely different reading of what constitutes useful agricultural R&D, and how to promote innovation, than what is imposed on Asia from Washington or Geneva. They emanate from the experiences of farmers in Asia and are rooted in a broader vision of national development that supports sustainable agriculture. IPRs emanate from the boardrooms of Japan, Europe and North America. With the onslaught of IPRs, the middle ground has disappeared and Asia's governments will have to decide which side they are on.

8

Seed Pricing and Costing

Price can be one of the most effective marketing tools available to a company. Price will be a more critical factor in marginal farming areas, where spending power is low, but less important where high yields can be obtained and farm produce can be sold profitably. Providing the benefits of the seed are understood, it is other factors, such as the availability of fertiliser and confidence in the produce market, rather than price that dominate the farmer's decision to purchase. Price varies from one market to another and between different segments in the same market.

The manager responsible for pricing a product must know how much more will be sold if the vice is lowered and, conversely. How much less will be sold if the price is increased. There is obviously a limit to what the farmer will pay as well as a limit to demand however low the price is set (unless seed is used for human consumption). As prices increase the point is reached where substitutes to bought seed, such as farm saved seed, may be used or the farmer may choose to plant a different crop.

Pricing strategies for a product or product line should be established on the basis of reaching short and long-term marketing objectives such as selling a certain quantity, achieving a certain market share or making a given margin over costs. However, prices are often set without taking into account the true cost of production and the effect which that may have on the competitive position of a product or product range.

Cost is a major factor in any discussion about price. Thus the costs involved in putting a bag of seed on the farm must be recorded, analysed and known to management. These costs will include the cost of the processed and packaged seed and the marketing costs associated with selling and distribution. Costs may be grouped according to the activities involved notably:

1. Seed production, involving procurement, processing and storage, quality control and certification.
2. Seed marketing, taking into account marketing, market research, advertising and promotion, sales and distribution.
3. Administration and finance.

For a company planning a seed production programme the working capital needed to procure and process seed has to be assured. If it is not to be financed out of existing resources then short-term loans are required to ensure that there is sufficient working capital. Seed held in stock at the various stages of processing also has to be financed. This is a significant cost item and there may be serious financial consequences for a business that has high stock levels.

The manner in which costs are allocated and presented will depend on the accounting system used. A simple presentation of a Profit and Loss Account demonstrates how income and costs relate. Elements which make up a Profit and Loss Account are described below:

- revenue: income from various sources such as sales, commissions or royalties
- sales: direct income from sales of seed commissions indirect income from sales made on behalf of a third party
- royalties: income earned from licensing varieties to a third party
- cost of goods: direct costs of procuring seed for sale plus treatments and packaging; may include processing costs depending on accounting policy
- gross margin: sales income less purchase costs (also expressed as a percentage); serves as a useful indicator of the earning power of the product or business
- expenses: company overhead costs associated with different activities such as production, sales and distribution, marketing, and administration
- trading profit gross: margin less expenses
- plant breeding: breeding, variety maintenance and trial costs
- gross profit: trading profit less plant breeding expenditure
- net profit after finance and tax: gross profit less finance and tax charges

The Profit and Loss Account can be presented for the business as a whole or for individual products or groups of products which may represent 'Profit Centres' within the business. Costs which are common to the whole business, e.g. the central management or the fixed cost of owning and operating a breeding station and processing plant, can be allocated across products. Although some products will be more profitable than others, and will be able to bear a greater share of the overheads, it is important to cost each product as honestly as possible for management control and decision-making purposes.

Pricing Policy

Seed pricing involves setting prices when a new product is launched or a new distribution channel is used. Also, decisions may need to be taken to change the price in response to competition and to the general market situation. In the public sector prices are often based on an economic pricing policy. Economic pricing considers the effect of seed price on the economy, taking into account the amount officials think farmers can afford to pay and the role of the seed industry in the development of agricultural production. Ideally, however, the public sector should follow a more commercial pricing policy which accounts for all costs and allows for an element of profit.

Some objectives in government seed pricing could be:

- to induce farmers to use certified seed of improved varieties in order to increase national production;
- to provide adequate incentives to seed producers to supply seed in sufficient quantity to meet demand;
- to encourage the development of private distribution channels;
- to implement government agro-economic policies.

The objectives of public-sector seed agencies are usually similar to those of government since the main purpose is to maximise seed use while achieving a marginal profit to finance the organisation. Institutional inefficiencies often mean that profits are not realised and the government is, in effect, financing a hidden subsidy to make up for the losses which cannot be covered by cost increases or operational improvements. Where subsidies can be justified they should be part of a declared policy of assistance provided to farmers for specific crop development programmes.

Subsidies should not be used to compensate for the inefficiency of seed supply organisations and should not discriminate against the private sector by only being available for seed supplied through the public sector. In some countries, the effect of subsidies is to create a great deal of uncertainty and this is a disincentive to private seed supply development. Government pricing policy should not undermine private enterprise in a mixed economy since the private sector will need to establish a price structure which will reflect the true cost of seed and meet its business objectives.

Subsidies may form part of transitional arrangements where the private sector is being encouraged to enter the market. This was the case when the seed market was liberalised in Turkey. The government arranged for subsidies to be paid to private companies with a phasing out over a five-year period. State-run organisations may continue to supply the high volume and low margin non-hybrid seeds, such as cereals, or seeds of public varieties while the private sector develops more profitable high margin and imported seeds. Some objectives in private sector seed pricing are likely to be:

– props maximisation which will be the long-term target although there may be many other shorter term considerations which will influence pricing policy, such as increasing market share and gaining acceptance of new products;

- price competition, may be achieved by setting a price that gives a competitive edge in the market place but may not be lower than that of a rival because other factors, such as service, will be contributing to a company's competitive advantage;
- a yield 01? investment which must be at least as good as other uses for investors' funds.

Pricing Strategies

Once a company's seed pricing objectives have been established, different pricing strategies must be considered. These include:

Low Price Strategy

Low price strategies are used where consumers respond very positively to small downward changes in price, but a company may not always gain from setting low prices as more efficient competitors may respond with similar price cuts. If the product is not particularly price sensitive then the net effect of a price reduction can simply mean a reduction in revenue. A company may be tempted to reduce its price where similar or substitute products are also sold or when there is an oversupply.

However, seeds can become devalued by selling them cheaply especially where there are real benefits associated with the product. Imported vegetable seeds are often chosen by farmers in preference to locally produced varieties in the belief that they are better because they are more expensive. It is therefore critically important to understand the likely response of the farmer when adopting a low price strategy.

Market Price Strategy

Where a few large companies dominate supply, products

tend to be similar (known in the seed industry as "me-too" varieties) and the role of price tends to be neutral, i.e. a market price is established.

High Price Strategy

This strategy can be used as a long- or short-term policy. In the case of the long-term policy the company will have identified a market segment for a high quality, value-added product such as graded and treated seed for precision drilling. A high price will reflect the exclusive image or added value of the product. A short-term, high-price policy takes advantage of a new product introduced onto the market, as may be the case with a new high-yielding variety where supply is limited.

Pricing Techniques

The important influences on pricing are cost, demand, prices of the product's main competitors and short-term sales targets.

Cost-plus Pricing

This method involves calculating the unit cost of a product and adding the appropriate profit margin to give a base price which might then be altered in relation to prevailing market conditions. While this seems a simple approach the fact that such pricing is production oriented and may therefore not reflect what is happening in the market place, makes it risky. A rigid application of cost-plus pricing may lead to price increases when demand is lower and reductions when demand is strong. This is the opposite of what should normally be done.

Contribution Pricing

This is a form of cost-plus pricing which involves

separating the different products that make up the product portfolio and allocating to them the direct costs associated with their production. The price is determined at a level which will generate revenues in excess of these costs, thereby contributing towards meeting business overheads. Individual products can be analysed in terms of their ability to cover their direct costs and contribute to overheads.

Competitive Pricing

Where there is market competition, costs cannot always be the determining factor in pricing. Here the nature and extent of competition will have a major influence on the price. If a product is faced with direct competition from similar products the price will be restrained. In contrast, when a product is faced by indirect competition from products in different sectors of the market there will be more scope to vary the price. This provides the possibility of using different strategies.

Short-term Pricing Techniques

Pricing can be a useful tool for pursuing short-term marketing and sales targets. When a new variety is launched higher prices can be set, providing the opportunity of earning higher returns from those farmers willing to pay the higher prices before seed becomes more widely available. Lower prices may be linked to promotional activities such as boosting sales of established varieties, creating interest in new ones, reducing high stocks and encouraging farmers to buy early.

Distributors' Margins

There are no fixed rules to apply, but the basis for setting a margin will depend on what is expected of the distributor and the acceptable final price to the consumer. Clearly, if the distributor is going to be actively involved in selling the seed and is expected to take a stock risk then the margin must afford adequate compensation. Seed margins have to be attractive enough to provide the dealer with an incentive to stock and sell.

Where there is competition, seed marketing companies compete by offering more attractive trading terms. This encourages dealers to stock their products and give them prominence. If farmers go to buy seed, and are undecided about the variety, the dealer will recommend seed from the most profitable supply source. If a seed company wishes to enter an exclusive arrangement with a dealer, such that seed of other companies will not be sold through the same outlet, then it is usual to provide a higher margin. The dealer will also have to be assured that the company is able to offer an adequate range of competitive products.

Whatever the mechanism used for setting prices these prices need publishing and publicising. Prices must be published in time for the selling season and in time for farmers to make their buying decisions. Frequently, situations arise in the public sector where all the parties involved in the price setting process fail to agree or the administration of the system is too slow. As a consequence, the sales campaign is delayed or there is uncertainty in the market causing seed to remain unsold. It is common to provide an internal price list for the seed company's sales staff giving details of margins, commissions and discounts and indicating the latitude they have when selling to the distributors.

Retail prices may be published as part of a catalogue or as a separate printed list. The advantage of a separate list is that it can be altered in response to market conditions more frequently than a printed catalogue. The distributors' price list should give details of: product group and variety name; package sizes and details plus package prices and the per kilogram price for comparison; prices for different seed preparations and treatments; the minimum unit of sale; discounts available and payment details. Some components of terms and conditions of sale:

1. Complaints procedure: the circumstances under which a complaint about seed quality will be considered.
2. Seed standards: regulations governing the supply of seed.
3. Latent defect: since seeds are supplied free of disease the company disclaims responsibility for subsequent infection when the seed is grown.
4. Definition of terms used to describe the variety response and performance: words such as resistance, immunity, tolerance and susceptibility are defined.
5. Plant variety protection: adjustment of prices to account for any royalty payments that are liable to be paid.
6. Published prices and quotations and subsequent alterations: explanation of what is included in the price and the right to alter quotations.
7. Force Majeure: covers factors outside the reasonable control of the supplier; standard exclusion clause covering the failure of a crop or delivery under such circumstances, such as a natural disaster, government action or civil commotion.

8. Damage delay or loss in transit: time limit and procedure modification
9. Transport charges and insurance: the supplier determines the delivery system. If he covers 'normal' delivery then any excess, e.g. express delivery, may be charged to the customer.
10. Payment: statement of standard payment terms and discounts.
11. Currency changes affecting the cost of seed this covers goods of foreign origin where there may he currency changes or the imposition of import taxes
12. Bankruptcy affecting the buyer and seller: legal position pertaining to bankruptcy of either party
13. Arbitration rules or legal jurisdiction under which disputes will he settled
14. Acceptance of terms: the placing of an order infers acceptance of these terms.
15. Seed supplied for crop production not seed production: disclaimer for performance of a subsequent crop grown from retained seed.
16. Property rights and payment: definition of the transfer of properly at the point at which payment is made in full.
    - date and period for which the prices apply;
    - minimum order time from supplier;
    - transport costs and arrangements if applicable;
    - insurance costs in transit if applicable;
    - appropriate contact names, addresses and numbers.

Terms and Conditions of Sale

These may be printed in catalogues, on price lists or on order and dispatch forms. They set out formally the basis on which the business will be conducted between the seller and the buyer. They also provide a reference point should there be any subsequent dispute. It should be understood that basic consumer protection rights cannot be avoided by simply writing disclaimers into the terms and conditions.

9

Supplying the Market

In making the decision to buy a particular variety from a given supplier the consumer will probably expect a whole range of benefits. These include those which relate to the performance of the product as well as less obvious benefits associated with the performance of the supplier.

A company may choose to distinguish the products it sells by identifying them with a brand name. Where a company has developed a strong name when a new variety is launched the farmer will recognise the name and will be more confident of trying the new variety. Where two companies are marketing the same or a similar variety it is these supplier performance features which will finally influence the purchase decision.

Product Portfolio

The term product portfolio is commonly used in the seed industry to refer to the range of products offered by a company. The product range can be described as the number of product lines, crop species, individual products or varieties of each line and brands. Companies can use brands to differentiate between seed quality levels and treatments as well as to differentiate markets for the same products.

Some companies specialise in certain seeds while others diversify their range of products to spread the business risk, achieve better utilisation of their assets or smooth out seasonal cash flows. A seed company will normally try to offer a wide range of seeds to capture as much of the customers' business as possible. The factors to be considered by seed companies in determining their range of products may include:

- the range of crops grown in the marketing area;
- the size of the individual seed market segments;
- market trends, e.g. whether the market is increasing, static or declining;
- the strength of the competition;
- the price farmers are willing to pay for seed, and there fore the likely return from supplying the seed;
- the factors in favour of the farmer purchasing seed, such as the difficulty of retaining his own seed or the choice of using hybrid seed;
- the source, ownership and exclusivity of varieties and variety development costs;
- seed production difficulties which might arise;
- the suitability and capacity of processing and storage facilities for the range of crops;
- the seasonality of crops;
- the implications on staff training, recruitment and administration of introducing new products or a new distribution system;
- government policy and support for different crops and seeds.

As well as thinking about the different product lines, a decision has to made about the number of individual varieties within a product line that can be maintained in the market. This decision will be influenced by overall market volume and the specific requirements of the identified market segments, such as:

- time to maturity;
- pest and disease resistance;
- quality features related to the end uses;
- agronomic features.

A commercial seed enterprise should constantly review the performance of the individual products which make up the product range since overall profitability may be positively or negatively affected by a few products. Cash generation relates not only to the volume traded but the gross margin earned, which is the difference between the cost of seed and the sale price.

Some seeds are more expensive to produce and this may not always be reflected in the price which can be charged. Also there is a cost to continuing the supply of pure seed stocks for commercial seed production. This may become too great when sales decline. The gross margin earning ability of products can be used to characterise the type of seed business and product portfolio offered. Products can be categorised based on performance or competitiveness and on owners/lip or exclusivity. The performance or competitiveness of products can be appraised as:

- superior or better than competitors' products;
- competitive, but no better than products offered by competitors;
- inferior or not as good as competitors' products.

Ownership or exclusivity refers to whether products are:

- public varieties which are available or accessible to all;
- proprietary varieties, the availability of which is controlled by the breeder or licensee.

A variety which is superior and sold on an exclusive basis would be expected to have higher earning potential than a competitive variety. Although a variety may be competitive in genetic terms, good quality, a strong brand name and effective promotion can create a sales advantage. It is common for breeding companies to make their own selections of standard varieties in order to create some identity and ownership of the variety. This is particularly true of vegetable varieties.

Life Cycle of a Product

There will always be a demand for new products. A product may last on the market only for one season, albeit a rare occurrence, or for many years. The concept of the product life cycle is an essential one for planning changes in marketing activities. The product life cycle recognises that products have a finite market life and charts their lifetime through various phases. In general a development phase exists for all products before they are launched onto the market. The life cycle can be broken down into five distinct stages as is shown in Figure 1.

In the introductory phase, growth is slow and volume is low because of limited awareness of the product's existence and perhaps a reluctance to accept an unproven product.

Sales then rise rapidly during the period of growth and profitability per unit of sale should reach a maximum as increased volume enables the benefits of economies of scale to be realised, with unit costs decreasing as fixed costs are spread over a greater number of packs of seeds.

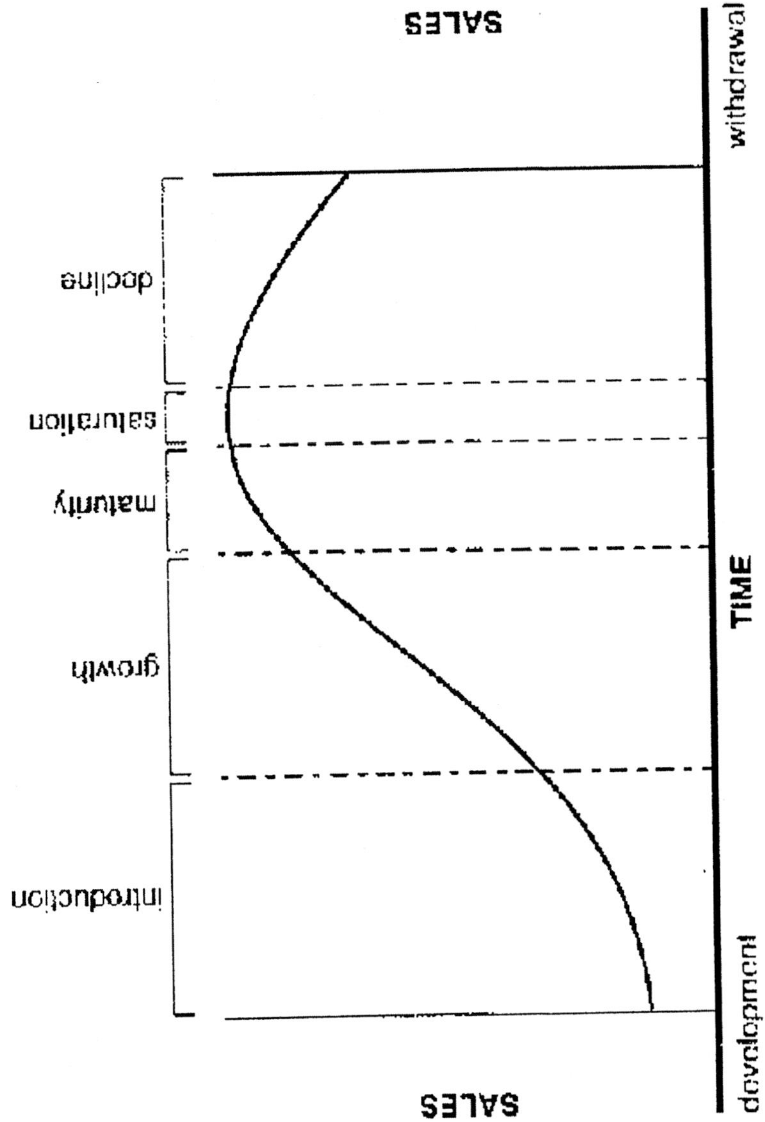

Figure 1. Stages in the product life cycle

Towards the end of this phase, competitors enter the market to promote their own, similar products and this reduces the rate of growth of sales. This period is known as maturity. The market then becomes saturated with the product and sales decline as competitive products erode market share, eventually leading to the withdrawal of the product when it is no longer profitable. The stages in the seed product life cycle are:

- development: breeding, selection, yield testing, official registration
- introduction: variety launch and promotion, field demonstrations and extension
- growth: increased awareness and acceptance of variety, build-up of commercial quantities of seed as dealers increase orders in response to demand created at the farm level
- maturity: growth in sales of the product slows down as maximum cover is reached; there will usually be a choice of varieties available and better performing varieties will be introduced
- saturation: maximum penetration has been reached and growth ceases
- decline: innovative farmers switch to a new variety while some stay for longer with tried and tested varieties
- withdrawal: the variety becomes outclassed; when it is no longer profitable to maintain and produce at very low volumes a decision to withdraw it has to be taken

To prolong the life of a product a company will need to alter the ingredients of its marketing mix. Changes might include:

- the improvement of the product arising from changes or modifications and an extension of the product line;
- the alteration of distribution patterns or the choice of different distribution channels (i.e. place);
- the use of price changes to stimulate sales or respond to competitors;
- change the style and emphasis of promotion.

Improvements to seed are made continuously through breeding and through Distinctness, Uniformity and Stability (DUS) testing by government agencies; thus any improvement in a variety may be considered to be a new product. The time scale of the life cycle stages will vary with different seed products ant markets. The development stage of a new variety may take 10-12 years, but the successive stages in its life cycle are dependent on variables such as the competition, the sophistication of the market and the pressure of new products in the breeding pipeline.

Most companies produce a range of products each of which has its own life cycle. Also, it is important to remember that new products may fail to meet registration criteria and existing ones may have to be withdrawn from the market prematurely. For example, resistance to disease could break down in a cereal variety due to the occurrence of a new strain of rust. Marketing programmes will have to be reviewed when such situations arise.

Product Marketing Plan

One aspect of marketing in a seed company is the design of a product marketing plan which, in turn, forms the basis of the production plan. This is how a market-driven organisation should operate. Unfortunately, in many non-commercial public sector agencies the reverse is the case. Those who do not sell the seed are making the production decisions. A three to five-year marketing plan should be created for each variety of seed. These plans should, in turn, be combined to form a product group plan.

It is important to think in terms of a three to five year time frame as seed from one generation is used to multiply the next generatior. The stock of early generation seed must therefore be sufficient for the production of the later commercial generations. Not only will the plan have to be communicated to the production department but also to the breeders. Successful seed supply requires a planned and integrated approach. If a variety is being produced under license from a foreign breeder, stock seed may have to be imported from abroad, adding a further stage in the process.

In a large company a product manager usually works closely in a team with plant breeders and staff from the sales and production sections in formulating the marketing plan. Even in a small organisation, where one person may have several functions, it is important to maintain this integrated approach. A standard internal production agreement form should be created by the marketing manager, giving the following details:

- variety, plus parental lines for hybrids;
- volume requirements with underlying assumptions, such as market shares;
- inventory policy, especially important for vegetables where stock may be heft to cover part of the following year's sales, or where stock of high margin seed is held to meet additional demand and for security of supply;

- packaging type and size;
- quality standards;
- labelling details;
- seed dressings;
- target cost and gross margin assumptions;
- target date for availability.

It is important that seed stocks are built up in advance of the launch of a new variety so that the sales growth phase is not slowed down by a shortage of seed. A delay of two or three years will mean that any yield advantage will be eroded by successive new varieties. It is also very easy to lose the momentum behind a marketing campaign. The dealers lose interest, the farmers turn to other varieties and the sales team are demotivated because they cannot deliver the seed. Work on varietal purity and early generation seed production would normally commence during the last few years of the trial period but building up commercial seed stocks prior to variety registration involves some risk.

Stock and Inventory Policy

It is important for a seed company to establish a stock policy based on product portfolio and marketing needs. There will always be some unsold stock, resulting from over production or lower than expected sales. Careful management and planning is needed to ensure that stock levels of commercial generation seed are kept to a minimum, thus avoiding losses and additional costs. As a general rule, of lower value, higher volume crops, such as cereals, and seeds of crops which are difficult to store, such as soybean, are produced to meet seasonal needs.

To ensure timely delivery a company may hold buffer stocks, particularly of its leading hybrid and higher margin varieties, or where sowing follows closely upon seed harvesting. The maintenance of adequate stock levels is vital to the success of vegetable seed businesses in particular since:

- there is often a continuous demand to cover seasonal and multiple cropping;
- there is a large number of product lines which have to be maintained and produced;
- seed of each line may not be produced in successive years;
- there are many biennial species where seed production will span two seasons;
- there may be difficulties in producing the seeds.

The production department should evaluate its variety plan in terms of:

- the date when the seed is required for sale in relation to the harvest period;
- the area required for each generation, allowing for the estimated loss of seed crops, contracts not honoured, crop and inspection failure and processing losses;
- the preferred production location;
- the availability of contract farmers;
- the harvesting period;
- transport and handling into the processing plant;
- processing and storage capacity;
- production risks;
- yield and cost estimates.

The marketing section should have some say in the production location. Where feasible, this should be related to the market location, and to arrangements for transport and the cost of transporting bagged seed from the plant to the point of sale.

Seed Packaging

Seed packaging helps to maintain the quality while facilitating handling and identification of the product. Packaging is a very powerful seed marketing tool and several factors have to be taken into account when deciding on appropriate packaging to be used:

Seed Quality

The quality of the seeds has to be maintained from the time of packing to the time of use by the farmer. The packing material and pack type chosen will depend on the nature of the product and the environment but packaging has to be resistant to moisture penetration, pest damage, adulteration, slipping in the stack and to rough handling.

It is important that the pack is adapted to market requirements in terms of size, weight and unit cost. Consideration must also be given to the mode and availability of transport from the point of purchase. A serious consequence of an over-large pack size is that the retailer will break bulk to sell the seed. This will provide the opportunity for deterioration and adulteration, and may invalidate the legal status of the labelling. Thus a number of factors need to be considered when planning for pack size. These relate the package size to the seed's value, its use and the area normally being sown.

Likewise, handling, portability and onward transport at the retail level are important so that retailers do not have to break bulk to sell the seed. Local knowledge can be important in determining if people are charged by weight or number of packages when transporting seed. Also, a bag that when empty has other uses may be a factor considered by the farmer in choosing which seed to buy.

Presentation

Presentation is a vital aspect of successful marketing. Packaging materials must be suitable for printing ant should be carefully designed to attract attention as well as being distinctive, in order to give the product and the supplier instant recognition. The packaging should form an association in the mind of the farmer between the seed and the supplier (known as the brand image) as well as providing information about the product and giving information on safety, storage and use of the seed. A clear pictorial representation is particularly important for vegetables. Finally, the package should provide as much protection from counterfeiting as is feasible.

Cost

A balance should be struck between cost, technical requirements and visual appearance of the packaging, in relation to the value of the seeds. If, in order to reduce costs, a standard bag or pack is used for a product line which requires a variety label or stamp to be applied this must be securely attached and be clear to read. Language and the use of graphic representation are also important considerations which will be dictated by regional and local factors. The promotional effect of packaging should not be underestimated.

Labelling

Information on the label should fulfil both the legal requirements of 'truthful labelling' and provide evidence of certification, where appropriate, as well as technical information about the product. Specific information provided should include:

- species, variety, germination, purity and contents;
- seed treatment and appropriate danger signs, plus warnings;
- seed lot number for tracing back to source;
- year of production and date labelled;
- expiry date of validity of certification, if required;
- statement invalidating quality assurance if the bag is tampered with.

Normally there will be a company label plus the official tag if the seed has been certified. The legal requirements vary from one country to another but usually state not only the technical information that should appear but print size, label size and colour. Colour coding is used for certification tags to denote the different generations. Labels should also be made of materials resistant to damage and have secure fixings. It is normal practice to place an additional label in the pack in case the one on the outside becomes detached. Product leaflets are also frequently included as a service to farmers.

10

Management of Distribution

Distribution is a key area of marketing and is a vital part of meeting the customers' needs and requirements. In a large seed organisation responsibilities are shared between those working in Sales, Inventory Control, Order Administration, Dispatch and Transport (ideally coordinated by the Marketing Department). Thus individual responsibilities need to be clearly defined. In small companies one person may fulfil all of these functions. Essentially, the marketing function takes over from production once the packaged seed has left primary storage. Distribution therefore covers the place element in the marketing mix and relates to getting:

- the right products
- in the right mix
- in the right quantity
- at the right time
- in the right place
- in the right condition
- at the right price
- under the right contractual terms

The route that seed follows to the consumer is often known as the marketing channel. There will obviously be marketing channels already in use but every business should continually reappraise the alternatives which means:

1. Setting distribution objectives.
2. Considering existing constraints.
3. Listing and evaluating the alternative systems.
4. Deciding on the best channels to use.

In conducting this appraisal, consideration should be given to the nature of the product, the distributors, the consumer and the competition. The product should be appraised by its:

- volume to weight ratio;
- unit package size and value;
- transport and protection requirements;
- handling characteristics (whether the product will be palletised or unpalletised); load size; requirements in terms of maintaining seed quality.

All the product's characteristics need to be taken into account. There is an enormous difference between moving fifty 50-kilogram sacks of wheat seed and fifty 50-gram packets of cabbage seed. High value, small packets will be more readily pilfered than SO-kilogram sacks thus making security a further consideration. Load and package size will have to be planned in relation to the availability of transport, road conditions, access and handling arrangements. The distributors should be evaluated in terms of:

- their existing product range and territory;

- the number of outlets needed to cover the market and the appropriateness of their locations;
- the location of the seed company's stores in relation to the wholesale or retail outlets;
- the size of the sales area allocated to an individual distributor, measured by the physical area and potential sales value;
- whether a single distributor should be given exclusive marketing rights; the capacity and quality of the available storage;
- the margin or commission and credit arrangements that will be required by the distributors;
- the need for training and marketing support;
- the handling of unsold stock and the need for a return system.

Seed consumers should be considered in terms of:

- the period when seeds are required and whether there is a single sowing period or, as in the case of vegetables, a more continuous demand;
- when seed is purchased and in what quantity;
- the most popular package sizes;
- the distance normally travelled between farm and retail outlet;
- the transport used by farmers to move the seeds to their farms;
- farmers' credit needs.

The competition should be appraised in terms of:

- which channels they use;
- the terms and conditions they offer their dealers;

- the capability of the company to match or improve on their level of service and support.

In planning physical distribution a balance has to be struck between the need to provide good customer service and the need to minimise costs. If a bag of seed does not get to the right place et the right time there is no sale and, as a consequence, the customer may not come back the following year. Farmers' demands are seasonal and they generally buy seed just before sowing time, rather than planning ahead, with the result that the transport and delivery system can be put under extreme pressure.

Intermediate storage between the seed company's stores and the retailers will therefore need to be considered to make the system more responsive, but this will add to the cost. Another approach is to encourage farmers to buy early so that stock can be moved to the dealers, thus easing the transport problem. For this purpose a 'buy early' promotion campaign could be run. Distribution is not just about physical product flow to the consumer. Several other movements are also involved. These all have to happen at the right time to make the system work effectively.

Seed Marketing Channels

Seed distribution can be carried out by government, public sector agencies, cooperatives and the private sector or, as is often the case, by a combination of all of these. Channels for seed marketing may be described as:

- direct: the seed producing organisation supplies the farmer directly
- single level: the seed producing organisation supplies the farmer through independent retail outlets

- multilevel: the seed producing organisation supplies a national distributor, wholesalers or regional distributors who, in turn, supply sub-distributors or the retail outlets

Direct Channels

Under this system the seed producing organisation maintains a sales division covering the sales area and supplying the farmer directly from central seed stores and a network of supply points. Some features of direct channel distribution are:

- the supplier has direct contact with the consumer;
- a high level of service and customer support can be maintained;
- direct control is maintained over the quality of the product;
- the upkeep of such a system can be expensive, with high fixed costs if a sales force is employed;
- a responsive management structure and well-motivated staff are required;
- where there are many staff involved in a direct sales organisation there can be an inbuilt inertia to change so the system may lack flexibility;
- the revenue necessary to pay for the high fixed costs will only come from having a wide product range and achieving good market shares or selling high value products such as horticultural seeds.

Where the public sector is the main supplier of agricultural inputs, a direct marketing system is often operated. The public sector must be aware of the need for an effective management structure, good communications systems and staff who are motivated and responsive to the needs of the consumer. Typically, however, such public sector organisations suffer from being 'passive' rather than 'active' marketing agents.

Private companies supplying field crop seeds are unlikely to be able to justify a direct sales organisation unless they have a monopoly on the market or are selling a broad product range in a developed market. Conversely, where a company has a considerable investment in proprietary, high-margin, low-volume products, such as vegetable seeds, direct marketing is a viable option.

Single-level Channels

With this system, the seed producing organisation supplies a network of retail outlets. In order to achieve national coverage, the producer may require intermediate storage in order to service these outlets adequately. The main features of this system are that:

- the seed supplier relies on the retailer for contact with the consumer;
- retail networks require strong service and support from the supplier;
- good administrative control must be provided by the sales management;
- the supplier's distribution system must be well organised and responsive;
- product quality at the retail level must be monitored for deterioration and adulteration and a return system should be considered;
- although the products may be well promoted, the supplier relies on the retailer to make the final sale.

Public-sector seed supply organisations are increasingly channelling sales through private dealer networks, in the interests of reducing costs and increasing sales. However, these dealer networks need effective support, and resources must be made available for marketing and promotion. An example is Indonesia where the sales of food crop seeds, produced through 20 processing units, have been transferred to a private sector network of 300 dealers and sub-dealers.

Multilevel Channels

Under this system the involvement of the seed producing organisation in physical distribution is minimised. This system is characterised by:

- the supplier having no direct contact with the consumer;
- products being strongly promoted in order to create demand;
- supplying seed to the distributors in sufficient time to achieve timely availability at the retail level;
- management ensuring that there is a good system of monitoring sales and obtaining feedback from the consumer;
- the distributor being interested only in the strongest selling lines.

If neither infrastructure nor the economy are well developed, national distributors may simply not be available and the seed producer will have to supply seed to regional wholesalers or distributors.

For farmers there are a number of sources available for the purchase of seed. These are:

- direct sales: the seed producer supplies the farmer directly from central seed stores and a network of his/her own supply points
- farmer producers: farmers with seed production contracts are licensed to supply other farmers within their zone of influence
- cooperatives: cooperatives act as 'farmer producers' and/or as suppliers of inputs to members
- farmer dealers: farmers act as dealers, supplying their neighbours; this can evolve into a highly developed system
- commission agents: these work directly with the producer or his/her intermediaries, passing on orders from the farmers
- grain merchants: traders involved in the seed and grain business who are also licensed seed producers
- crop buyers: collectors and crop or commodity traders who provide a point of contact with farmers and can be used to market seed
- retail store dealers: town and village dealers who retail a range of agricultural inputs, with the larger operators possibly having sub-dealers
- industrial processors: processors interested in specific crops including oilseed crushers and vegetable canners, who may have an interest in supplying seed as part of a growing contract or integrated production system
- cold store operators: potato cold store operators trade potato seed since they deal directly with the growers and have the appropriate storage

- consumer outlets: garages, shops and supermarkets (are best suited to display small packets of seed)
- mail order: suitable for low volume high value products such as vegetables and flowers

Although government extension outlets are not strictly retail outlets, seed is sometimes supplied to the farmer through government sponsored agencies and departments which administer crop or regional development and credit programmes.

Storage and Transport

There are several reasons why seed is stored:

- to allow the efficient management of seed handling and processing;
- to cover the natural time gap between seed harvest and sowing;
- to enable sufficient stocks to be carried in the distribution system;
- to carry over unsold stock from season to season;
- to provide security of supply (buffer stocks) to meet fluctuations in demand and supply and meet the agreed inventory policy;
- to provide sufficient stock seed for future production requirements.

Assuming that seed is harvested at maturity with satisfactory germination and vigour, it will become subject to a natural process of deterioration over time, the rate of decline being influenced by several factors such as moisture content, packaging, treatments and storage. These factors must be controlled to ensure that seed bought by farmers is in satisfactory condition and has retained its potential for high performance. It is very important that storage conditions are satisfactory and that seed is regularly monitored for both internal as well as external deterioration.

Dealers frequently sell fertiliser as well as seeds and it is imperative that seed is not stored alongside fertiliser. Fertiliser attracts moisture from the atmosphere creating damp conditions that damage seeds. Separate arrangements have to be made for the transport and distribution of potato seed, which requires special cool storage conditions. Storage problems and seed quality loss are caused by:

- high humidity and high temperature causing loss of germination and vigour;
- water, causing direct damage, increasing humidity and promoting fungal attack;
- insects and pests (birds and rodents) causing direct damage and spillage;
- cross contamination from fertilisers, chemicals and toxic materials;
- pilfering of seed due to the insecurity of the store.

To avoid such storage problems a company should consider constructing or renting high quality buildings which may be both fumigated and ventilated, with concrete floors, waterproof roofs, moisture-proof walls, good roof space above stack height, power and light. The location chosen should have adequate drainage and not be prone to flooding. Seed should be stacked off floor level and apart from other products. Holes in roofs, walls and under doors need to be avoided to prevent pests from entering the store.

The stores should be secure with an efficient stock control system in place; and regular checks of buildings and seed storage conditions should be carried out. Although ownership of the seed may have passed to the dealer it is the name of the supplying organisation which is carried on the bag. The marketing manager in the supplying organisation must be satisfied that minimum storage standards can be met by the distributors, allowing for the length of time seed is expected to be in store. Reference could be made to these minimum standards in the representation agreements.

In planning storage a judgment must be made concerning peak holding capacity and carry-over requirements, the capital cost of building and the availability and the cost of space which can be rented, and the off-take rate during the sales season. The latter will depend on distance, transport, demand patterns and storage at the point of sale. If the seed organisation has a regional structure, a network of regional seed stores should be provided from which distributors and retail sales points can be quickly supplied. Apart from concerns about security and basic protection, physical storage requirements will depend on the amount of time that the seed is likely to be held.

Generally, seed can be moved back to central stores which have the required specifications after the selling season, to ensure that quality is maintained over longer periods of time. This will also make retesting and relabelling more convenient. A policy decision will have to be made regarding the provision of a return system for dealers. The supplying organisation can be expected to have comprehensive insurance for goods held in its own stores but special cover may have to be arranged for goods in transit if the seed-supplying organisation undertakes delivery.

Alternatively, seed can be sold ex-store with responsibility passing to the customer. The decision whether to supply ex-store or deliver can only be made in relation to the local situation but will be influenced by the product type, customer base and the competition.

Distribution and Sales Management

Sales Service

In order for distribution and sales to be managed effectively a sound management and reporting structure is vital at every level. Within the marketing organisation the sales service functions are directly concerned with the operational aspects of seed distribution. Central sales and distribution functions are:

- central sales management;
- order administration and preparation;
- transport;
- dispatch;
- stock records and inventory control;
- sales administration and invoicing (credit control).

While the field sales force consists of:

- regional sales management;
- technical representatives;
- safes representatives.

Assuming that seed is distributed on a regional basis through a dealer system the marketing manager should:

- allocate responsibility for major customers within the organisation in order that they may receive special attention;

- define the sales territories of the area sales managers, salesmen and dealers;
- know what the potential seed requirement is by the type of seed in each territory;
- agree sales targets when setting the forecast and budget with those responsible for the territory;
- schedule dealer visit and support programme with salesmen;
- insist on activity reports from the salesmen and arrange regular meetings;
- establish a regular reporting system for monitoring sales and stock availability, both at the point of sale and at the supply locations;
- introduce a sales staff incentive scheme in the form of bonuses or gifts linked to individual sales performance.

Administration System

Every organisation needs to develop a sales administration system which would include the following steps:

- order receipt: entering the order into the order administration system
- order validation: checking details, customer status and carrying out credit checks
- stock allocation: checking that stock is available and adjusting stock records
- order alteration: refering back, if necessary, to salesmen and customer
- dispatch allocation: allocating packing date and rotation and dispatch number

- order preparation: withdrawing stock and adjusting stock records
- order dispatch: notifying salesman and/or customer when to expect delivery
- invoice: sending by post, or by special order if leash-on-delivery' is being used
- payment receipt: entering payment receipts in the accounting system
- credit control: collecting over due accounts, where necessary

Reference has been made to the fact that useful marketing information can be generated from invoices. Sales administration generates management control information, such as sales progress and stock update reports, and triggers action if stock shortages develop in the distribution system. The importance of accurate stock control and record-keeping throughout the system should not be underestimated. This should include seed at all stages of bulk storage, processing and awaiting sale.

Information that may effect planning, e.g. the effect of drought, the timing of rains or possible disruption to the transport system must also flow in from the sales regions. Obviously, good communications are vital if the system is to respond quickly to potential sales opportunities.

Selection of Dealers

The number and distribution of sales' points and dealers is influenced by the cover required to adequately service the market. A judgment will have to be made on how best to service the farmers in a region and achieve the sales and financial objectives of the organisation.

It is important to make an assessment of the general activity of the dealer since, as well as selling seed, the dealer is the primary contact point with the market. There is no point in a company servicing inactive dealers. Once selected they should agree to minimum targets for a mix of products. The dealership should be worth holding so the dealer will work to achieve targets rather than risk losing his dealership.

It is recommended practice to sign representation agreements with distributors and dealers. It is important that the dealer be willing to participate in company training programmes. The dealer should be trained, not only in the technical and agronomic aspects of the product range, but in product presentation, selling and storage. There will also be a requirement for the dealer to follow various administrative and record-keeping procedures.

The farmer may need a credit before being able to buy inputs. Credit can come from several sources but competition between seed companies may lead to credit being extended to farmers through the dealers. Dealers may therefore be required to operate a credit system supported by the seed company.

11

Crop Marketing Services

Input supply can be usefully subdivided into three types of services:

- Fertilisers and chemicals
- Seeds and planting materials
- Machinery and equipment.

Inputs, equipment, and crops are mainly private goods because most are excludable and rivalrous. Indeed, production and distribution of agricultural inputs and equipment, as well as crop marketing, are typical private sector businesses in most OECD countries. In principle, it should be possible to decentralise these services in developing countries through market liberalisation, encouragement of private and voluntary sector organisations to enter service provision and improved efficiency and/or divestment of public sector organisations. However, for effective government disengagement, markets have to be well developed, there has to be an absence of general or specific market failures, and no other grounds for government intervention such as merit good status or income redistribution.

Factors Affecting Demand and Supply

Fertilisers and Chemicals

Superficially, fertiliser distribution is an ideal service for private sector provision, as fertiliser can be considered as a pure private good being both rivalrous and excludable. The demand for fertiliser and chemicals is a derived demand and will be influenced by the price and profitability of the crop as well as the price of the input. However, fertiliser use often increases the risk faced by farmers if rainfall is low and/or crop prices are below expectations. This will tend to make the demand for fertiliser unstable as well as seasonal.

With imperfect and incomplete finance markets, credit-constrained farmers will find it difficult to purchase fertiliser unless new channels of credit provision are made available to them. This is one conceivable disadvantage of scrapping single channel marketing systems. Although a temporary problem, exchange rate devaluations in the early days of liberalisation combined with the removal of subsidies often led to substantial increases in domestic fertiliser prices and marked falls in effective demand.

For low-income countries it is sometimes argued that food security stimulated by fertiliser use on food crops generates positive externalities and thus, in principle, a case may be made for government intervention in the form of fertiliser subsidies. This is particularly true if the demand for fertiliser is price elastic and reducing the price of fertiliser leads to a marked increase in food production and food security.

Imperfect information

There are two types of imperfect information relating to

fertiliser and chemical use. The first relates to the quality of the products. The effects of fertiliser applications, in particular, are often not seen for several months. It is therefore quite feasible for an unscrupulous trader to sell inferior quality products to farmers. The second relates to appropriate advice relating to applications. If this is not available, input use is likely to be sub-optimal or even ineffective. However, for fertiliser applications this advice tends to be crop- and location-specific as it is closely linked to soil and climatic conditions.

Like all information, it has public good characteristics that suggest that the government should be involved in its provision. With pesticides and herbicides, incorrect use can generate serious negative externalities in the form of threats to human health and environmental damage that justify some form of government intervention in provision.

Seeds and Planting Materials

Seed supply is a complex operation consisting of three major components:

- Research into new and improved types of seeds
- The physical supply of seeds
- Regulation including:
  a) the management of variety testing in public sector plant breeding
  b) variety regulation (registration, performance testing and release)
  c) seed quality control consisting of seed certification (verification of genetic quality) and seed testing (analytical purity and germination capacity).

In pre-reform situations public sector organisations are frequently responsible for all three functions, but there is no economic reason why this should be the case. Nevertheless, the nature of seed technology and the characteristics of the product suggest that the public sector is likely to continue playing a role in the provision of the research and regulation components.

Seed technology is rivalrous but only in the case of hybrid varieties is excludable. Open-pollinated varieties (OPVs) can be reproduced by farmers themselves and passed on through informal seed distribution mechanisms. This makes them common pool goods. While private sector firms are willing to conduct research into developing new types of hybrid seed, they will often not find it attractive to develop new OPV seeds. Exceptionally, they may have a clear advantage in terms of quality and reliability of supply that enables them to capture a significant share of the market.

In some developed countries plant breeders' rights give sufficient protection to make private sector provision of OPVs a viable proposition but it is debatable whether they would be appropriate or enforceable in developing countries. In small and poor countries with small potential seeds markets it is likely that the public sector, or non-profit organisations, will always play an important role to overcome this particular problem of market failure.

One problem facing potential entrants to the seed supply sector is the strong seasonality of demand that means large stocks of perishable seed need to be carried. This ties up working capital but investment in adequate storage facilities is also required. The private sector also requires a level playing field and this is unlikely to be achieved if either the public sector or NGOs are subsidising seed production or sales.

Several aspects of seed regulation require at least some form of input from the public sector to overcome potential market failure problems. Seed certification must be sponsored by the public sector although it can be performed by a private organisation. The government must also regulate seed testing, although companies that are trying to establish a reputation for themselves are inclined to apply their own adequate seed testing procedures, and associations of seed producers may provide this service for their members.

Equipment Supply

There is a potential problem of market failure relating to imperfect and asymmetric information. As with fertiliser, it may be difficult for a farmer to assess the inherent quality of machinery and this creates particular difficulty when items involve substantial investment and purchases are only made infrequently.

Crop Marketing

There are three potential market failure problems with agricultural produce marketing that need to be taken into account when considering decentralisation. First, it is inherently risky because of unpredictable variations in output that cause marked price and income fluctuations. These in turn may cause food insecurity. Second, there may be positive externalities related to food security that justify some form of government intervention. Finally, spatial dispersion means that small and remote farmers may suffer from a lack of information and exploitation by traders.

Decentralisation

In principle it should be possible to decentralise most

input and equipment supply and crop marketing services in developing countries through market liberalisation, encouragement of private and voluntary sector organisations to enter service provision and improved efficiency and/or divestment of public sector organisations. This, indeed, has already occurred in many countries. State 'shrinkage' has played a role in the measures undertaken so far and has included actions such as:

- Liquidation of autonomous crop marketing public agents
- Withdrawal of the extension services from input supply
- Liquidation of bankrupt agricultural banks heavily engaged in extending credit for input purchase to non-repaying farmers
- Halting subsidy programmes, which led to the liquidation of state supported cooperatives.

Even though the private sector has assumed a much larger role in input supply and crop marketing, governments at the central and local levels have an important role to play in creating an enabling environment for private sector activities.

The development of a competitive market for agricultural inputs requires inter alia that:

- Equal opportunities to trade are given to all potential suppliers.
- Adequate credit facilities are available to private traders.
- Producers/suppliers selling products that embody special technical characteristics are protected against unfair competition.

– Farmers have an adequate knowledge about the quality of the products that they buy.

Naturally, for an effectively competitive inputs market to achieve an efficient allocation of resources in the agricultural economy of a country, an equally effectively competitive market for crops must be in place. Four main conditions must be met for this to happen:

– Deregulation and liberalisation of the national crops market, including imports and exchange rate and a least distorting and transparent taxation/subsidy regime.

– Adequate market information available to producers and traders.

– Adequate access to credit by traders and producers, to enable the latter to finance their stocks on the farm prior to sale. This will improve their negotiating power vis-à-vis traders.

– An adequate network of transport infrastructure in the rural areas.

The development of functioning private markets is not a short-term objective. In many developing countries, particularly small countries at the lower end of the scale in terms of income, there is hardly what can be called 'a private sector' capable of important new initiatives. It takes time for this to come about. In larger countries with more developed economies, the private sector is often dominated by large traders who concentrate on import/export operations and in supplying urban areas, where the volume of business is large and profit margins significantly higher than in rural areas.

As a result, in many rural areas of larger and more developed countries the situation is not dissimilar to that of smaller and less developed countries. Under these circumstances the policies aimed at developing functioning rural markets must be prompted by a long-term vision. New rules and other measures must be introduced and implemented in a coherent manner and on a permanent basis. This is a major challenge that is not always faced adequately.

In fact, the persistence of the negative effects of market failures and the many factors related to the power configuration of the public agencies involved have often provided justification for continued government intervention in the agricultural markets as 'interim measures'. Some interim measures have actually represented partial reversal of reform policies, discouraged private initiatives and seriously jeopardised the effectiveness of the reform.

Private enterprise will respond over time to meet an effective demand for agricultural inputs. This will be generated from the development and promotion of crop technologies that bring about significant, not marginal, returns to farmers. This will often require actions by both the private and public sectors. Large trading companies engaged in export crop processing and input producers both have a general interest in promoting the growth of demand for inputs, because it brings about more crops to buy, not just more inputs to sell. These private enterprises may go beyond the assessment of existing markets and often have the resources to do so.

A dynamic fertiliser market, for example, needs to be fostered by continued research on soil fertility, on crop responses under different ecological conditions, on adequate crop protection practices and products, on variety development, cropping practices, etc. In the case of 'cash crops' input suppliers and crop buyers do get involved in research and extension. This is not only the case of large-scale multinational companies. In Kenya, for example, several medium-size private companies engaged in seed production and in export of horticultural products are now involved in research and extension activities.

To promote increased effective demand by commercially oriented farmers, a crop approach to research and extension is often sufficient to identify which technical packages interest producers, stimulate more demand for inputs and production of more crops of interest to buyers. For the other category of farmers, matters are much more complex. Here, a farming system approach, continuous participatory diagnosis of problems and on farm adaptive research are required.

Government intervention is justified when private enterprise shows a strong tendency to be limited to production and distribution of products that embody a high degree of monopoly, such as chemicals or hybrid seeds. In these cases governments may legitimately support the introduction of alternative technologies, such as integrated pest management (IPM), and encourage producers of truthfully-labelled seeds of composite varieties, and of disease-free planting material of root and tuber crops, which can be easily reproduced by small scale farmers.

Spreading the know-how on IPM may be a publicly-supported research and extension activity, justified on grounds of mitigating negative externalities and of enhancing competition in the plant protection technology market. Supporting producers of composite seeds and of disease-free planting material fills a gap in supplies and stimulates competition with hybrid seed suppliers. It also responds to the needs of a different category of users.

The most effective way of providing government support depends on country- and location-specific conditions. However, in the majority of cases, some form of devolution to the private and voluntary sectors would be useful, with the public sector retaining such functions as providing technical advice, supply of basic seeds, supervision of truthful labelling by producers, and implementing phytosanitary controls at government research laboratories. Local governments do not appear to be an adequate locus for decision making in matters related to input supply and crop marketing services, particularly with respect to subsidy management, because of spillover effects. For example, products subsidised in an area can be sold at market price in another area.

A strong case can be made for central governments to support capacity building and training of CSOs (farmers' associations, genuine cooperatives, NGOs) in handling input supply and crop marketing services. Apex organisations in the voluntary sector can play an important role in moderating the impact of asymmetric information, which affects farmers and particularly poor farmers in a negative way with respect to both input purchasing and crop sales.

A most important contribution of government to mitigate rural market failures is to improve transport infrastructure. Many development specialists would share the view that if all the financial and human resources spent on fostering government direct intervention in crop marketing, input supply, and related credit operations were spent on improving rural transport infrastructure and on designing effective mechanisms for the maintenance of secondary and feeder roads, then the history of agricultural and rural development might have recorded a different performance in developing countries.

Decentralisation may provide important potential solutions to the provision of transport infrastructure. In most countries road construction and maintenance is the responsibility of public works departments (PWD). Normally, however, the PWD is not responsible for rural roads, which creates a serious institutional gap through the absence of a clear allocation of authority and resources in this domain. Planning trunk roads by PWD is generally influenced by the importance of urban centres, with little account being taken of the agricultural potential of rural areas.

Traffic counts are used to establish priorities and these record existing situations. This invariably means that high potential agricultural areas with inadequate transport infrastructure produce much less, and therefore generate much less traffic, than they would with better infrastructure. This is well known to agricultural economists and planners and there is ample empirical evidence of the impact of rural road programmes on crop and livestock production. However, strong arguments against giving priority to feeder road construction are the difficult logistics and the high maintenance costs, particularly in tropical and equatorial environments.

Devolution of responsibility for planning, construction and maintenance of rural roads is one option tried in several countries with World Bank support. In some cases, local governments (regional or district level) have been devolved financial resources on a matching grant basis for rural road construction and maintenance. These have been financed from a share of the central government fiscal revenue from road users (for example, a given percentage of the tax on petrol and diesel) coupled with the authority to raise local levies from road users.

The local governments then contract out design, construction and maintenance to various private enterprises. The deconcentrated units of technical ministries provide the necessary support to the local governments in contracting and supervision of consultants, and/or contractors' performance. The advantages of this option are to:

- Provide a stable source of funding to local governments
- Stimulate their capacity to raise local taxes and, presumably, the willingness to pay taxes which taxpayers know are earmarked to provide better services to them
- Entrust planning to the level that is best aware of requirements and potential benefits and to promote local civil work enterprises in the private sector.

There are however drawbacks to this approach that need to be considered and, if possible, overcome. These include:

- Limited technical capacity of local governments
- Inadequate resources or simply resistance of deconcentrated units of technical ministries to provide the required assistance
- Interference by local pressure groups with priority setting
- Low revenue collection from road users' levies.

In practice, it will take time to make the new system functional and performance is unlikely to be the same in all local governments.

A complementary option is to provide funds to finance, through CSOs, local community projects on a matching grant basis under partnership arrangements.

This would be more appropriate when road projects benefit single villages rather than a number of villages, which is the domain of the district on account of jurisdictional spillover. Such small projects could be supported on a cost-sharing basis with the local community's share, in cash or labour, paid in advance to provide proof of stakeholders' commitment. The argument in favour of this option is that if local people are free to select the project they desire they will select a road project whose benefits are not shared with other communities. Having willingly invested their own resources in its construction there is a higher probability that they will take care of the road maintenance.

Another important contribution of government to improve the performance of private markets is the provision of better communication systems. Mass communication media (radio and television) are increasingly used by public extension organisations. Technology breakthroughs in telephone communications mean, for example, that small portable cellular phones fuelled by batteries can be purchased and operated by farmers (or groups of farmers) at reasonable costs. This would allow them to acquire very valuable information on crop prices, market demands, etc., on a private basis thus reducing the disadvantages of asymmetric information. However, for this to be possible, the networks of such services need to cover rural areas.

An important aspect of crop marketing that also affects input markets concerns price fluctuations, which are a major problem for agricultural producers. At the global level, commodity markets have developed very sophisticated institutions with a view to attracting private investors and moderating the negative impact of sharp and erratic fluctuations in the price of agricultural commodities. Examples are global commodity information services, global commodity exchanges, financial products such as trading in futures and ample commercial storage facilities.

The overall impact has been positive, but price fluctuations continue to be a feature of the international agricultural commodity markets. The experience of most developing countries with price stabilisation schemes and buffer stocks have been fairly negative, with the result that policy reform advocates have argued convincingly in favour of ending such schemes. The current opinion is that government intervention in export crops markets is not advisable because little can be done by a national government to influence global markets beyond what global markets institutions already do and the risk of wasteful use of limited financial resource is considerable.

In domestic markets, crop price fluctuations are more pronounced with sharp seasonal fluctuations in food crop prices compounding the impact of inter-annual fluctuations. Price instability is one of the main risks faced by agricultural producers, and the absence of adequate market infrastructure and institutions, particularly for food crops, is a major market failure in developing countries. Furthermore, failure to maintain national food security is often a threat to political stability.

The issue confronting decentralisation reform designers is how to introduce effective mechanisms aimed at moderating agricultural price fluctuations, with a minimum of direct government involvement. There are some examples of successful management of floor price policy by government agents.

BULOG, an Indonesian government organisation, controls minimum paddy prices through open market operations involving less than 3 percent of the national crop. It does this through good management of a deconcentrated monitoring of local markets, and of an effective network of purchasing agents, coupled with adequate resources. Admittedly, paddy is an irrigated crop, with smaller production fluctuations than rainfed crops, which makes price stabilisation easier.

Nevertheless the BULOG experience is worth keeping in mind. However, grain stock management and price stabilisation, at any level, require high management skills, transparent and accountable management, no corruption, and good experience of markets reactions and behaviour. Moreover, no such scheme can effectively deal with the impact of long lasting droughts or exceptional calamities.

Decentralisation policies include other successful experiences. These concern, for example, the promotion of community storage schemes at village level in several African countries, some of which have managed to effectively improve producers' prices. Overall, however, the experience of these projects is mixed. Some have been wrongly designed, with an emphasis on physical storage facility construction rather than working capital requirements, and without a workable link to the sources of commercial finance. Many have been located in deficit areas for food security purposes, rather than marketing improvement.

The approach has a better chance of working in grain surplus areas where farmers' stocks of grains can fetch higher prices during the lean season. Group storage has considerable advantages, including the possibility of obtaining credit from commercial banks on the basis of 'bonded stock' procedures, improved market information, and lower transport cost through bulk conveyance to markets. Coordination with the central government stock management policy is required, to avoid decisions about selling public stocks at the wrong time undermining the viability of village storage operations.

A Financing Role

Generally speaking, there is little justification for government to subsidise inputs and equipment. It is sometimes alleged that there is 'inadequate' use but this is often because technical 'requirements' are confused with effective demand. There are several instances where special crop production programmes associated with input subsidy schemes have performed well, but whether this was primarily determined by input subsidies or by favourable market conditions, adequate infrastructure, and appropriate technologies is far from clear. On the other hand, there are many examples of overestimation of the potential demand, because many important factors determining demand are invariably underestimated by agricultural development planners. Among these are:

- High risk factors of various nature confronting producers
- Poor crop responses to inputs in specific local agronomic conditions
- The limited share of the cash economy in the farmer household budgets
- Better alternative investment opportunities for employment of surplus cash resources
- Lack of cash to purchase basic household needs, etc.

Regulatory Issues

Even if the government divests itself of its responsibilities for producing, delivering and financing input and crop-marketing services, it still has an important role in providing a regulatory framework with rules that govern the trade in agricultural inputs, equipment, and crops. This framework should foster the effective functioning of markets and moderate the effect of market failures. The revision of this regulatory framework is an important part of the decentralisation process.

Trade regulations

In a decentralised system of governance, and in pursuit of liberal economic policies, regulations governing trade play a vital role in creating a satisfactory enabling framework. With regard to input and equipment supply and crop marketing services the main issues that need to be covered include:

- Ensuring a competitive environment in the market for a specific good or service
- Ensuring that users of goods and services are informed about the quality of products they buy
- Certifying the quality of the products or the competence of the suppliers where quality is not easily discernible by visual inspection
- Preventing or regulating the use and sale of products that may cause negative externalities
- Collecting information for statistical and policy purposes.

Trade regulations may be handled at different levels of governance. Typically the central government establishes the regulations or at least the framework within which detailed regulations must be formulated by other agents, and may delegate the power of taking action for enforcement to lower levels of governance. In some cases the authority to formulate regulations may be devolved to lower levels.

Trade regulations are particularly important in agricultural input supply to protect farmers from frauds by unscrupulous suppliers, and to prevent or regulate negative externalities. Enacting adequate rules is not a simple matter when complex technical issues are involved. Enforcement is not always easy. Good simple regulations vigorously enforced can be highly beneficial.

Decentralised enforcement, and some degree of devolution to professional and consumers' associations, may help making rules more effective. However, too many rules, or vague, confused often contradictory rules may have devastating effects. Over-regulation may obtain opposite results to the declared objectives of the regulating authority. Typically the scope for decentralisation decreases the more numerous are the regulations, and the more complex the procedures which must be applied. At the same time the scope for abuse by public administration officers increases. Three particular issues related to trade regulation deserve some more attention:

- The procedures required to obtain permits and trading licences
- The prevention of negative externalities
- The protection of users' rights.

Trade licences

Trade licences are enforced in every country across the world. Good governance requires that the procedures to obtain a licence are simple, transparent and equitable. However, often the criteria for obtaining a licence are opaque and there are unreasonable delays in granting a licence. In agriculture, the fees charged and the documentation required by the administration to issue a licence can be serious handicaps for small traders. The principle of subsidiarity suggests that responsibility for issuing licences can usually be undertaken by deconcentrated local units of the central administration, or devolved to local governments, with a view to cutting 'red tape' and delays in processing the applications.

Market liberalisation and privatisation in many countries have not always been accompanied by the reform of administrative procedures. Even when far reaching changes in policy and procedures have been introduced, widespread and transparent information has not always followed. The failure to simplify procedures and/or adequately inform people about changes does not reduce the delays, the high transaction costs (of a legal and illegal nature), and the other impediments which limit the effectiveness of liberal economic policies.

As a result, many rent-seeking positions in bureaucracies are not seriously challenged and the role of private enterprise will fall short of expectations. In a democratic system of governance, the public authorities have a precise responsibility to make rules clearly understandable and widely known, well beyond the publication in official journals that are sometimes difficult to find even in capital cities in developing countries. Deconcentration and devolution, when local managers are effectively accountable to a local constituency, may help to reduce the risk to some extent.

Negative externalities

This objective requires that input users are adequately informed about the potential negative effects of the products that they intend to use on the sustainability of their own resource. This is essentially an extension message problem, which, because of conflict of interest, cannot be entrusted to the product suppliers. It also needs users to be fully and very clearly informed about the specific characteristics and the adverse effects of inappropriate use of a product, such as endangering the user's health (in the case of poisonous products, for example), or the health of his plants and animals.

In part, this can be achieved by rules that insist on adequate labelling of products and on full disclosure of information by suppliers in product marketing. Government has a general policing responsibility in this respect vis-à-vis traders and manufacturers, which needs to be forcefully implemented. The extension service has a specific function of warning uneducated farmers about dangerous products circulating in the market (legally or illegally).

Consumers' rights

This is particularly important in the case of seeds, since product quality is an essential element of the price set by suppliers and a consumer's decision to buy. However, the external characteristics of the product often do not reveal product quality, making fraud easy. Government therefore has the responsibility for regulating the quality of the seeds traded in the market. The rules enacted depend on decisions about the strategies to be followed to enhance quality control, and the related organisational consequences such as delegation to autonomous agents in accordance with the specialisation principle.

There is a different view emerging about the role of government in performance and quality control, based on neoclassical economics arguments and on some empirical evidence about the cost and benefits of the regulatory function. Regulations have a direct cost for government and suppliers (government employees cost money, suppliers dealing with procedures spend money), that may or may not be commensurate with benefits. Some regulations may yield negative net benefits. For example, delaying the introduction of new products for a long time, until all tests of performance and quality are carried out, deprives users of considerable gains which they may have made by using the product, and discourages private suppliers to seek introducing new products.

12

The Indian Seed Industry

Past Status of Seed Industry

The National Seed Corporation was established in 1963. The Government of India enacted the Seeds Act in 1966 to regulate the growing seed industry. The sixties were the most eventful times for Indian agriculture, not only because of introduction of high-yielding cereals, particularly wheat and rice but also for many other positive developments related to seed such as, constitution of Seed Review Team, enactment of Seeds Act, 1966 and formation of National Commission on Agriculture. This was the period, during which the private sector significantly stepped into the seed business.

The Seeds Act stipulated that seeds should conform to a minimum stipulated level of physical and genetic purity and assured percentage germination either by compulsory labelling or voluntary certification. Further, the Act provided a system for seed quality control through independent State Seed Certification Agencies which were placed under the control of state departments of agriculture. The eighties witnessed two more important policy developments for the seed industry, viz. granting of permission to MRTP/FERA companies for investment in the seed sector in 1987 and the introduction of 'New Policy' on seed development in 1988.

The 1991 Industrial Policy made a radical departure from the earlier policy on foreign investment. Under this policy seed production was identified as a 'high priority industry'. The New Policy on Seed Development greatly liberalised import of vegetable and flower seeds in general and seeds of other commodities in a restricted manner and also encouraged multinational seed companies to enter the seed business. More than 24 companies initiated research and development activities and have made substantial commitments for investment on research and development in response to this policy initiative.

The investments are expected to increase with increasing volumes of seeds of proprietary hybrids and preparedness of farmers to pay higher price for quality seed. A draft Seeds Act 2001 is being finalised on the basis of the recommendations of Seed Policy Review Group. It would replace the existing Seeds Act of 1966 and Seed (Control) Order of 1983. The proposed legislation features establishment of National Seeds Board (NSB) and compulsory registration of any seed with the board before sowing or planting could be done for commercial purposes.

Present Status of the Seed Industry

India's seed industry has grown in size and level of performance over the past four decades. Both private and public sector companies/corporations are involved with the production of seed. The public sector component comprises two central corporations, viz. National Seed Corporation (NSC) and State Farm Corporation of India (SFCI) and 13 State Seed Corporations. The private sector comprises around 150 seed companies, which include national and multinational companies and other seed producing/selling companies.

The industry has made impressive strides from a modest beginning in seed production in 1962-63 to over 5 lakh hectares by 1995-96. The quantum of seed produced and sold has gone up by five times from 14 lakh quintals to 70 lakh quintals during the corresponding period. In 1990-91 the area planted with bought seed was about 10.35%. The total bought seed in 1990-91 was estimated at around 5.91 lakh tonnes valued at Rs 679.80 crores (tables 1 and 2). This seed component in 1990-91 comprised of proprietary hybrids, public-bred hybrids and open-pollinated varieties.

Table 1. Indian seed market (Quantity in tonnes)

Year	Saved seed	Bought seed	Total
1998–99	8,953,523	864,899	9,818,422
1990–91	5,125,299	591,200	5,716,499
Quantity increase over 1990–91	3,828,224	273,699	4,101,923

In terms of quantity and value, seed of open-pollinated varieties was the largest followed in order by public hybrids and proprietary hybrids. Seed of the proprietary hybrids formed a significant portion of the total seed market. In terms of quantity, although proprietary hybrids had only 32.34% share of the market, in terms of value the share was 76%. In contrast to the 1991 scenario, the estimates in 1998-99 presented a different picture with proprietary hybrids growing at the expense of the public hybrids.

Table 2. Indian seed market 1990-91 and 1998-99 (Rs in crores)

Category	1990-91	1998-99
Proprietary hybrids	95.00	636.00
Public-bred hybrids	124.65	245.00
Varieties	460.15	1368.55
Grand total	679.80	2249.55

The area planted to bought seed increased by 3% over that of 1990-91 and the market size expanded significantly in terms of quantity and value. The total market for purchased seed was 8.64 lakh tons valued at Rs 2249 crores. The component of proprietary hybrid seed was estimated to be around 51,314 tonnes in 1998-99 as against 19,300 tons in 1990-91 and valued at Rs 636 crores as against Rs 95 crores respectively. The volume of public bred hybrids came down to 38,704 tons in 1998-99 as against 59,671 tons in 1990-91.

The volume of seed of open pollinated varieties (OPV) increased by 51% to 774,881 tonnes (tables 3 and 4). The present contribution of OPV in the total bought seed market segment has expanded indicating greater use of bought seed by farmers. The price paid by farmers for all hybrid seeds was higher than that in 1990-91. The trend is suggestive that price of seed is not considered a constraint in usage by the farmers, if the seed ensures higher return through higher productivity and other value added traits.

Table 5 gives data on the quantity of seeds marketed in 1990-91 and 1998-99 for cereals, oilseeds, fibres, potato and pulses. It is seen that the quantity in saved seeds significantly reduced in 1998-99 compared to 1990-91 in case of oilseeds and fibres whereas it increased in cereals and potato. A reverse trend is seen in case of bought seeds. The quantities increased significantly in 1998-99 compared to 1990-91 in all categories except potatoes; the increase is almost one and a half times.

Table 3. Composition of Indian seed market – 1998–99. Bought seed

Category	Proprietary hybrid	Public hybrid	Variety	Total
Cereals	43,287 (15,600)	30,208 (52171)	496,841 (297,329)	570,336 (365,100)
Oilseeds	5233 (2200)	2720 (1800)	142,298 (76,300)	150,251 (80,300)
Fibres	2475 (1500)	5776 (5700)	25,280 (17,400)	33,531 (24,600)
Pulses	– (-)	– (-)	41,900 (-)	41,900 (-)
Vegetables	319 (-)	– (-)	1662 (17,000)	1981.11 (17,000)
Potato (seed)	– (-)	– (-)	66,900 (70,000)	66,900 (70,000)
Others	– (-)	– (-)	– (34,200)	– (34,200)
Grand total	51,314 (19,300)	38,704 (59,671)	774,881 (512,229)	864,899.11 (591,200)

In case of vegetables and pulses, the bought seeds were 1981.11 tonnes and 41,900 tonnes respectively in 1998-99 compared to nil in 1990-91. Table 6 gives a break-up of saved seeds and bought seeds in five cereal crops, viz. jowar, bajra, maize, paddy and wheat. The increase in saved seeds in cereals in 1998-99 is contributed only by wheat while in other crops the quantity of saved seeds decreased in 1998-99 compared to 1990-91. There is a significant increase in the sale of proprietary hybrids in case of jowar, bajra and maize, particularly in bajra (~ t 8 times) and maize (3 times). In case of jowar the increase is around 20%.

Table 4. Composition of Indian seed market. Value of marketed seeds over different categories of crops in 1998–99 and 1990–91 (Rs in crore)

Category	Proprietary hybrid	Public	Variety hybrid	Total
Cereals	254 (26)	90.00 (63.15)	560.00 (153.55)	904.00 (242.70)
Oilseeds	109 (26)	20.00 (4.50)	312.60 (145.60)	441.60 (176.10)
Fibres	138 (57.00)	135.00 (33)	84.20 (24.00)	357.20 (114.00)
Vegetables	135 (10)	- -	217.35 (65.00)	352.35 (75.00)
Pulses	- -	- -	127.40 (33.00)	127.40 (33.00)
Potato (seed)	- -	- -	67.00 -	67.00 -
Grand total	636 (95)	245.00 (24.65)	1368.55 (460.15)	2249.55 (679.80)

Table 5. Composition of Indian seed market. Quantity of the seeds marketed over different categories of crops in 1998–99 and 1990–91 (Quantity in tonnes)

Category	Saved seed	Bought seed	Total
Cereals	4,208,162 (3,592,806)	570,336 (365,100)	4,778,498 (3,957,906)
Oilseeds	1,165,552 (1,313,680)	150,251 (80,300)	1,315,803 (1,393,980)
Fibres	16,709 (21,602)	33,531 (24,600)	50,240 (46,202)
Vegetables	- -	1981.11	1981.11
Potato (seeds)	3,563,100 (171,680)	66,900 (70,000)	3,630,000 (241,680)
Pulses	- -	41,900 -	41,900 -
Grand total	8,953,523 (5,125,299)	864,899 (591,200)	9,818,422 (5,716,499)

Only 537 tonnes of hybrid rice seeds are sold in 1998-99. In case of public bred hybrids, in contrast to proprietary hybrids of private companies, sales in jowar reduced to 18,545 tonnes from 30,400 tonnes in 1990-91. A similar decrease was observed in bajra; in 1998-99 quantity sold was reduced by 3418 tonnes from the total sale of 10,100 tonnes in 1990-91.

The sales of public bred maize hybrids remained at 11671 tonnes in both years for which a comparison has been made here. The scenario in the sales of varieties was different. In case of wheat and paddy there has been increase in the sales of varieties in 1998-99 compared to 1990-91. There were no sales of maize varieties in 1998-99 when 5729 tonnes were sold in 1990-91. It was seen that there was significant reduction in sales of varieties in bajra in 1998-99 whereas there was an increase in case of jowar varieties.

Table 6. Composition of Indian seed market. Cereal seeds marketed in 1998-99 and 1990-91 (Quantity in tonnes)

Category	Saved seed	Proprietary hybrid	Public-bred hybrid	Variety	Total
Jowar	48,195 (63,256)	7400 (6200)	11,855 (30,400)	3425 (2100)	70,875 (101,956)
Bajra	38,445 (49,806)	11,350 (1400)	6682 (10,100)	3523 (6500)	60,000 (67,806)
Maize	55,793 (63,336)	24,000 (8000)	11,671 (11,671)	- (5729)	91,464 (88,736)
Paddy	1,138,654 (1,144,408)	537 -	- -	200,402 -	1,339,593 -
Wheat	2,927,075 (2,272,000)	- -	- -	289,491 (145,000)	3,216,566 (2,417.000)
Grand total	4,208,162 (3,592,806)	43,287 (15,600)	30,208 (52,171)	496,841 (297,329)	4,778,498 (3,957,906)

Table 7. Composition of Indian seed market. Oilseeds marketed in 1998–99 and 1990–91 (Quantity in tonnes)

Category	Saved seed	Proprietary	Public-bred hybrid	Variety hybrid	Total
Sunflower	4755 (2354)	4900 (2200)	0 (0)	1943 (4900)	11,598 (9454)
Mustard	29,469 (27,791)	0 (0)	0 (0)	9823 (6600)	39,292 (34,391)
Soybean	430,153 (186,996)	0 (0)	0 (0)	53,165 (9100)	483,318 (196,096)
Groundnut	684,500 (1,091,075)	0 (0)	0 (0)	72,700 (55,000)	75,720 (1,146,075)
Castor	1322 (5464)	333 (0)	2720 (1800)	2067 (700)	6442 (7964)
Safflower	7988 (0)	0 (0)	0 (0)	1600 (0)	9588 (0)
Sesame	7365 (0)	0 (0)	0 (0)	1000 (0)	8365 (0)
Grand total	1,165,552 (1,313,680)	5233 (2200)	2720 (1800)	142,298 (76,300)	1,315,803 (1,393,980)

Table 7 gives figures on the sales of oilseed crops in 1998-99 and 1990-91. There is a definite increase in the sales of saved seeds in sunflower, mustard, soybean, safflower and sesame in 1998-99 compared to 1990-91. As a matter of fact, there were no sales of safflower and sesame in 1990-91. There has been a significant decrease in sales in 1998-99 in groundnut and castor compared to 1990-91. There were no sales of proprietary hybrids in case of mustard, soybean, groundnut, safflower, sesame in both the years as there was no technology for hybrid seed production in these crops.

In castor only 333 tonnes of proprietary hybrid were sold in 1998-99 compared to no sales in 1990-91. In sunflower there has been a definite increase in the sale of proprietary hybrids in 1998-99 (more than double) than in 1990-91. No public bred hybrids were sold in both the years except in castor. In castor 2700 tonnes of public bred hybrids were sold in 1998-99 compared to 1800 in 1990-91.

As far as varieties are concerned, there has been a decrease in sales in 1998-99 in case of sunflower (from 4900 tonnes to 1943) whereas in the case of mustard, soybean, groundnut and castor there has been definite increase in sales in 1998-99 compared to 1990-91. There were no sales of varieties in safflower and sesame in 1990-91, while in 1998-99, 1600 tonnes of safflower and 1000 tonnes of sesame seed were sold.

Future Status of Seed Industry

Accounting for approximately 30% of the national GDP, agriculture is the backbone of Indian economy. It is the source of livelihood for over 70% of its population. Having the largest arable area (170 million ha), India ranks second only to USA in sheer size of agriculture. By virtue of its large arable land area, sizeable irrigated area, rich agri-biodiversity, diverse agro climate and welldeveloped research system, the country has all the potential to emerge as a global power in agriculture.

The impressive growth registered in agricultural production in general and food grains in particular during the last 30 years has made the country self-sufficient in cereal grain with a sizeable surplus which can be exported. Even to remain where we are today in terms of level of per capita consumption of food, the country has to add another 40 million tonnes by 2010.

With no more arable land and productivity of major crop plants plateauing, the prospects of achieving the target especially with the aid of currently available technologies is a challenging proposition. Many of the problems that impede the productivity of our varieties and hybrids have defied solution through conventional breeding approach. These include widespread moisture stress (> 65% of the area particularly under rainfed and dryland conditions), expanding salinity, new pests and biotypes of higher virulence and poor shelf-life.

There is thus a distinct need for innovative technologies to find solutions to existing and emerging problems and thereby increase the overall productivity and stability of our major crops. Unlike in developed countries, population growth in India is far in excess of its growth in agricultural production warranting continued inputs to achieve a steady increase in food production. The route to increase in production lies through improved agronomic practices and availability of high quality seed.

At the current pace of growth, meeting the future food grain demand would be an uphill task. The new technologies for increasing yield should also be sustainable in the long run. The high-yielding technology that heralded the Green Revolution has, no doubt, rescued the country from chronic food deficiency and starvation but it has had its adverse effects too. The high input cultivation of rice and wheat has led to excessive water use and eroded soil quality; indiscriminate use of chemical pesticides has led to pesticide resistance making pest management increasingly difficult.

Any scope for pest control through host plant resistance is becoming limited on account of shrinking sources of resistance. Weed infestation causes heavy crop losses, if not controlled in time. The estimates of losses caused due to pests and weeds range between 10% and 40% but in some cases the losses could be much more. Beyond herbicides, which are weed specific, there are no means to manage the wide weed spectrum.

Limited variability for yield-related traits is slowing down the progress in yield enhancement. Hybrid technology, though a potential technological option, has not yet become a reality in several crop plants for want of stable cytoplasmic male sterility-fertility restoration system, as is found and exploited in sorghum, pearl-millet, sunflower and rice. In crops like wheat, heterosis is being commercially exploited in India from this year.

In crops like Indian mustard and in pulses like pigeonpea and safflower though exploitable hybrid vigour is quite sizeable, for want of stable male sterility/ restorer systems and lack of economic hybrid seed production technology, the scope for increasing yield has been limited. Many of our staple food are characterised by deficiency of one or the other nutrients and excessive dependence on the same has led to nutrition deficiencyrelated health disorders.

Plant breeders can rectify problems in a crop only when there is variability available for the desired character within the compatible species complex. Transfer of useful traits from distantly related species which do not sexually cross with the crop plant is not possible through conventional recombination breeding procedures. Considering that many problems still remain unsolved and that the currently available technologies are inadequate to solve them, there is need for alternate technologies.

Recombinant DNA technology that enables movement of genes of interest across sexual incompatibility barriers is one approach plant scientists are relying upon worldwide today to find genetic solutions to specific problems. Recognising the potential of genetic engineering and biotechnology and its relevance to India, the Ministry of Science and Technology established the Department of Biotechnology (DBT) in 1986, exclusively to develop and apply biotechnological approaches in agriculture, animal science and human health.

The Ninth Plan outlay of DBT was around at Rs 1026 crores, more than double that in the Eighth Plan (Rs 427 crores). The first transgenic Bt cotton underwent field-testing in 1995. Today 185 institutions, which include both public research institutions and private research laboratories, are engaged in transgenic research. Currently, transgenic research is being done on several field crops, viz. cotton, Indian mustard, corn, potato, tobacco and rice and in vegetable crops namely tomato, brinjal, cauliflower, cabbage, chillies and bell pepper.

The problems receiving priority attention include insect pest control, hybridisation systems and nutrition improvement. Genetically engineered hybrids and hybrids with unique characteristics such as pest resistance are of special interest to the private sector institutions, as they provide a degree of certainty, offsetting the risks to their investments in biotechnology. Two transgenics now under field-testing, viz. Bt cotton hybrids against bollworm complex and Indian mustard (Brassica juncea) for exploitation of hybrid vigour are of this kind.

Several large and medium-seed companies with turnovers ranging from Rs 35 crores to 100 crores are intensively pursuing full-fledged in-house agro-biotech research and development either on their own or through joint ventures with foreign companies. The fact that 23 private sector institutions have today their own Institutional Biosafety Committee (IBSC), which is mandatory under the guidelines for institutes engaged in genetic engineering research, is indicative that private companies are as serious and interested as public institutions in pursuing transgenic research.

Transgenics will have a major impact on seed business. For instance, as new varieties with improved performance enter the market, shares of individual varieties will shift quickly. Dramatic increase in the annual research expenditures of private companies engaged in biotechnology research is yet another indicator to the increasing involvement of private sector in biotechnology research.

A strong regulatory system for assessing biosafety of genetically engineered plants and food items before they are released in the environment is mandatory. A 3 tier regulatory system for field-testing of transgenic plants structured on the basis of guidelines issued by the DBT under the Environment Protection Act 1986 is in place. The rules for the manufacture, use, import, export and storage of hazardous microorganisms, genetically engineered organisms or cells were framed in 1989 under the Environment (Protection) Act of 1986.

Biosafety guidelines were formulated by RDAC (Recombinant DNA Advisory Committee) in 1990 and were adopted by the Government. They were revised in 1994 and 1998 incorporating allergenicity and toxicity evaluation of transgenic material. The guidelines incorporating changes up to August 1998 have been published recently. These guidelines prescribe the codes for experimentation and field-testing of transgenic material for assessing safety. It is pertinent that no testing of transgenics can be done without permission of the RCGM under the Environment Protection Act.

The Act provides penalties including prosecution for violation of the Act. The Indian regulatory system is a 3-tier structure. It comprises the following:

- Institutional Biosafety Committee (IBSC), set-up at each institution for monitoring institute level research in genetically modified organisms.
- Review Committee on Genetic Manipulation (RCGM) set-up at DBT to monitor ongoing research activities in GMOs. A Monitoring and Evaluation Committee (MEC), comprising agricultural scientists, was constituted in July 1998 by RCGM to monitor and supervise field trials permitted by the government.
- Genetic Engineering Approval Committee (GEAC) in the Ministry of Environment and Forests has been setup to authorise large-scale trials and environmental release of genetically modified organisms.

Biotechnology research requires substantial investment and time to get a product commercialised. It is becoming increasingly difficult for even large companies to pursue biotechnology research alone because of large investments needed and the inevitability of using already protected genes and protocols in developing transgenics. These limitations/hurdles necessitate collaborative research/ joint ventures at national/international levels today than at any point of time before. At the national level, scope for such collaborative research between advanced public institutions and prospective private companies is unlimited.

The Government of India has invested substantially for biotechnology development, the impact of which is seen in the emergence of several lead laboratories in various aspects of genetic engineering research including discovery of novel genes. Cloning of high protein AmAgene from Amaranthus spp. and its successful intro into potato by the Centre for Plant Genome Research, Delhi, the refinement of barnase-barstar system and its use in Indian .mustard for exploitation of hybrid vigour by the University of Delhi South Campus, identification of a salt-tolerance gene from a mangrove species by the M.S. Swaminathan Research Foundation, Chennai, are some of the original pieces of work done in India. This kind of research creates intellectual property for the institutions involved and provide leverage to get access to technologies from other technology holders.

What we lack at present is the framework/system for bringing together researchers in public institutions and the private seed industry. In the national interest, the evolution of a viable system for joint ventures should be given priority attention.

The presence of a stringent regulatory system for assessing biosafety of transgenics is in the general interest of the country. However, if the system is cumbersome and time-consuming, the very purpose for which it was created will be defeated. The system in place at present is rationally planned and structured. But the need for an applicant to deal with four different organisations, viz. Department of Biotechnology, Ministry of Environment, the Indian Council of Agricultural Research and several state governments for getting the entries evaluated under the 3-tier system, is daunting in itself and may scare away industry from investing in the development of transgenics.

In the absence of referral laboratories for evaluating the transgenic products for biosafety, the applicant is required today to come up with such information on its own. The current regulatory system requires coordination among 3-4 ministries, viz. Ministry of Health, Ministry of Agriculture, Ministry of Environment and Forests, and Ministry of Science and Technology.

For assessing the agronomic superiority of the transgenics, large scale multi-location trials are necessary. Though it is being practised under the 3-tier system, there is scope for improvement. When the transgenic variety is sent for field-testing, multi-location trials could be conducted simultaneously by the ICAR if required, so that the time taken for testing is reduced. There is a need to simplify the system towards a single window clearance so that the applicant need not deal with multiple institutions as indicated above.

Need to Control Illegal Activity

This is a great challenge to all concerned including the governments at central and state levels. An effective control and monitoring system can genuinely promote biotechnology. Any individual in our democratic set-up is at liberty to make a statement, take potshots at Government Institutions and indulge in illegal activities like uprooting experimental material undergoing testing/ evaluation.

It is imperative that the Government machinery with greater assertiveness checks such unlawful activities perpetrated by vested interests so as to ensure adequate testing/evaluation of the genetically modified crops. There is an immediate need to address these problems objectively and on priority for ensuring larger and rapid acceptance and adoption of the technology which is of immense value to our country and which can contribute towards the country's growth as a global agricultural power.

Biotechnology is the science of tomorrow. It has the potential to find solutions to problems that have defied solution so far. Biotechnology ventures need substantial upfront investment, hard and concerted work and intense interphase with regulatory system. For this, coupled with changing market conditions, it would therefore be wise and prudent for majority of the private companies to forge links with public research institutions, especially universities. Collaboration with transnationals is a hotly debated issue. There is no reason why collaboration with international institutions and transnationals should be shunned. Such ventures may be in high national interest.

Collaborations with advanced laboratories enable development and delivery of a technology in the shortest time possible. This would enable faster development of products leading to generation of resources which could be invested in industry for enhancing future capabilities. Given the complexity of development and regulations in the area of transgenic crops, collaboration with appropriate laboratories would be most cost effective and time saving. There are many areas and issues relevant to Indian agriculture where joint ventures would prove rewarding.

Development of resistance to leaf curl virus in cotton and tomato, yellow stem borer in rice, pod borer in pigeonpea, male sterility/restorer system in oilseed Brassica, nutrition enrichment in rice and potato, tolerance to drought in rainfed crops, etc. are some of the areas where novel solutions would help immensely. Revenues can only be maintained through savings on costs and increasing market shares and sales by collaborating with other organisations in the business. The alliances may include joint ventures, acquisitions etc.

A sense of partnership has to be created between government and private sector institutions to ensure that biotechnology takes big strides for advancement of Indian agriculture. Capital intensive biotechnology research generates not only transgenics of value but also valuable knowledge and skills. Their protection through appropriate legislative mechanism is of utmost importance to motivate more and more entrepreneurs to invest in this area of science. It is gratifying, that the Parliament of India has recently approved the Protection of Plant Varieties and Farmers Rights Act.

Speedy operationalisation/implementation of the same is critical for protection of national wealth. IPR in patents or PVP form will not only provide a legislative framework but also a suitable environment for large-scale upfront investment in biotechnology research. The products developed by R&D efforts in recognised private research establishments would be protected and unethical practices in contract farming could be prevented. Education and creation of awareness among farmers and the general public on the benefits and risks associated with transgenic crops is important to blunt the negative campaign on transgenics. The government along with all stakeholders should make all-out efforts to disseminate such knowledge.

13

Marketing Reforms in India

Most agricultural commodity markets generally operate under the normal forces of demand and supply. However, with a view to protecting farmers' interest and to encourage them to increase production, the Government of India also fixes minimum support/ statutory prices for some crops and makes arrangements for their purchase on state account whenever their price falls below the support level.

The role of Government normally is limited to protecting the interests of producers and consumers, only in respect of wage goods, mass consumption goods and essential goods. The role of Government is promoting organised marketing of agricultural commodities in the country through a network of regulated markets.

To achieve an efficient system of buying and selling of agricultural commodities, most of the state Governments and Union Territories have enacted legislations (APMC Act) to provide for regulation of agricultural produce markets. The basic objective of setting up of network of physical markets has been to ensure reasonable gain to the farmers by creating environment in markets for fair play of supply and demand forces, regulate market practices and attain transparency in transactions.

With a view to coping up with the need to handle increasing agricultural production, the number of regulated markets have also been increasing in the country. While by the end of 1950, there were 286 regulated markets in the country, today the number stands at 7521 (31.3.2005). The Central Government advised all the State Governments to enact Marketing Legislation to promote competitive and transparent transactional methods to protect the interests of the farmers. Barring a few, most of the States and Union Territories embarked upon a massive programme of regulation of markets after enacting the legislation. Most of these regulated markets are wholesale markets.

There are in all 7293 wholesale markets in the country. Besides, the country has 27294 rural periodical markets, about 15% of which function under the ambit of regulation. The advent of regulated markets has helped in mitigating the market handicaps of producers/sellers at the wholesale assembling level. But, the rural periodic markets in general, and the tribal markets in particular, remained out of its developmental ambit.

The area served by each market across the States reveals large variations. The area served per regulated market varies from 74 sq km in Punjab to 2257 sq km in Assam. On an average, a regulated market serves 459 sq km area in the country which is quite high. Farmers have to travel long distances with their produce to avail the facility of regulated markets. The National Commission on Agriculture had recommended that the facility of regulated market should be available to the farmers with in a radius of 5 km and if this is considered a bench mark, the command area of a market should not exceed 80 sq km.

However, in the existing scenario, except Delhi, Punjab, Chandigarh and Pondicherry, in no State, the density of regulated markets is close to the norm. Auction platforms are needed in market for settlement of price of the produce in a congenial atmosphere between buyers and sellers. Both covered and open auction platforms exist in only two-thirds of the regulated markets. Some commodities when brought for sale contain higher moisture than desired level and hence there should be a space for drying.

Presently only one-fourth of the markets have common drying yards. Trader modules viz. shop, godown and platform in front of shop exist in 63% of the markets. Cold storage units are needed in the markets where perishable commodities are brought for sale. They are brought for sale only in a few markets. The cold storage units exist only in 9% of the markets and grading facilities exist in less than one-third of the markets. The basic facilities viz. internal roads, boundary walls, electric lights, loading and unloading facilities and weighing equipment are available in more than 80% of the markets. Farmers' rest houses exist in more than half of the regulated markets. It is evident from the above that there is considerable gap in the facilities available in the market yards.

Limitations of Agricultural Markets

The purpose of regulation of agricultural markets was to protect farmers from the exploitation of intermediaries and traders and also to ensure better prices and timely payment for his produce. Over a period of time these markets have, however, acquired the status of restrictive and monoplistic markets, providing no help in direct and free marketing, organised retailing, smooth raw material supplies to agro–processing, competitive trading, information exchange and adoption of innovative marketing systems and technologies. Farmer cannot sell his produce directly in bulk except on retail basis to the consumers.

Farmers have to bring their produce to the Market yard. Exporters, processors and retail chain operators can not get desired quality and quantity of produce for their business due to restrictions on direct marketing. The processor can not buy the produce at the processing plant or at the warehouse. The produce is required to be transported from the farm to the market yard and then only it can be purchased and taken to the plant. There is thus an enormous increase in the cost of marketing and the farmer end up getting a low price for his produce.

Under the APMC Act, only State Governments are permitted to set up markets. Monopolistic practices and modalities of the State-controlled markets have prevented private investment in the sector. The licensing of traders in the regulated markets has led to the monopoly of the licensed traders acting as a major entry barrier for a new entrepreneur. The traders, commission agents and other functionaries organise themselves into associations, which generally do not allow easy entry of new persons, stifling the very spirit of competitive functioning.

Agriculture sector needs well functioning markets to drive growth, employment and economic prosperity in rural areas of the country. In order to provide dynamism and efficiency into the marketing system, large investments are required for the development of post harvest and cold chain infrastructure nearer to the farmers' field. Projection of production and marketable surplus of various farm products was recently assessed by an Task Force set up by the Ministry of Agriculture which estimated that an investment of Rs.12,230 crore in next 10th Plan would be necessary for infrastructure development for agricultural marketing.

A major portion of this investment is expected from the private sector, for which an appropriate regulatory and policy environment is necessary. Alongside, enabling policies need to be put in place to encourage procurement of agricultural commodities directly from farmers' field and to establish effective linkage between the farm production and the retail chain and food processing industries. Towards this end, the Inter-Ministerial Task Force on Agricultural Marketing Reforms constituted by this Ministry in its report of 28.06.2002 has made the following important recommendations:

i. Promotion of competitive agricultural markets in private and cooperative sectors, direct marketing and contract farming programmes by amending the State Agricultural Produce Marketing Regulation Acts and to provide central assistance for the development of marketing infrastructure subject to such deregulation and reforms;

ii. Progressive dismantling of controls and regulations under the Essential Commodities Act to remove all restrictions on production, supply, storage and movement of, and trade and commerce in respect of all agricultural commodities;

iii. Substantial step up in flow of institutional credit to farmers for marketing of crops (pledge financing) to enhance their holding capacity to obtain remunerative price for their produce;

iv. Expand availability of warehousing services in rural areas by introducing negotiable warehousing receipt system for agricultural commodities; and

v. Allow futures trading in all agricultural commodities to improve price risk management and facilitate price discovery by amending the Forward Contracts (Regulation) Act, 1952.

The recommendations contained in these Reports were discussed with the State Governments at a National Conference on 27th September, 2002 and later by a Standing committee of State Ministers on 29th January, 2003. In the Conference as well as the Standing Committee, State governments expressed the view that reforms in the agricultural marketing sector were necessary to move away from a regime of controls to one of regulation and competition.

In view of liberalisation of trade and emergence of global markets, it was necessary to promote development of a competitive marketing infrastructure in the country and to bring about professionalism in the management of existing market yards and market fee structure. While promoting the alternative marketing structure, however, Government needs to put in place adequate safeguards to avoid any exploitation of farmers by the private trade and industries. For this, there was a need to formulate a model legislation on agricultural marketing.

The Ministry of Agriculture accordingly formulated a model law on agricultural marketing in consultation with the States Governments. The draft model legislation provides for establishment of Private Markets/Yards, Direct Purchase Centres, Consumer/Farmers Markets for direct sale and promotion of Public Private Partnership in the management and development of agricultural markets in the country. It also provides for separate constitution for Special Markets for Commodities like Onions, Fruits, vegetables, Flowers etc.

A separate Chapter has been included in the legislation to regulate and promote contract-farming arrangements in the country. It provides for prohibition of commission agency in any transaction of agricultural commodities with the producers. It redefines the role of present Agricultural Produce Market Committee to promote alternative marketing system, contract farming, direct marketing and farmers/consumers markets. It also redefines the role of State Agricultural Marketing Boards to promote standardisation, grading, quality certification, market led extension and training of farmers and market functionaries in marketing related areas.

Provision has also been made in the Act for constitution of State Agricultural Produce Marketing Standards Bureau for promotion of Grading, Standardisation and Quality Certification of agricultural produce. This would facilitate pledge financing, E-trading, direct purchasing, export, forward/future trading and introduction of negotiable warehousing receipt system in respect of agricultural commodities.

Implementation of Marketing Reforms

A. Implementation of Model Act on Agricultural Marketing: The following steps have been taken to persuade the States to bring changes in the APMC Act on the lines of the Model Act:

   i) National level meetings were organised with the State Governments at Delhi on 07.01.2004 and at Bangalore on 19.11.2004.

   ii) Follow up letter from Union Agriculture Minister sent to State Ministers In-charge of Agricultural Marketing for amending the APMC Act on 16th July, 2004 and again on

February, 2005 and to the Chief Ministers on 25-5-05.

iii) A new Central Sector Scheme to provide investment subsidy on market infrastructure development projects implemented in November, 2004. Central assistance under the scheme is to be provided in those States that amend the APMC Act on the lines of the Model Act. An amount of Rs.25 crore was also released to NABARD/ NCDC to provide investment subsidy to eligible projects through banks in March, 2005.

iv) Several States have initiated steps for amending the APMC Act.

B. Contract Farming: Contract farming has been prevalent in various parts of the country for commercial crops like sugarcane, cotton, tea, coffee, etc. The concept has, however, gained importance in recent times in the wake of economic liberalisation. The main feature of contract farming is that farmers grow selected crops under a buy back agreement with an agency engaged in trading or processing.

There are many success stories on contract farming such as potato, tomato, groundnut and chilli in Punjab, Safflower in Madhya Pradesh, oil palm in Andhra Pradesh, seed production contracts for hybrids seed companies in Karnataka, cotton in Tamil Nadu and Maharashtra etc. which helped the growers in realisation of better returns for their produce. In our country contract farming has considerable potential where small and marginal farmers can no longer be competitive without access to modern technologies and support.

The contractual agreement with the farmer provides access to production services and credit as well as knowledge of new technology. Pricing arrangements can significantly reduce the risk and uncertainty of market place. Small-scale farmers are frequently reluctant to adopt new technologies because of the possible risks and costs involved. In contract farming, private agribusiness will usually offer improved methods and technologies because it has a direct economic interest in improving farmers' production to meet its needs.

In many instances, the larger companies provide their own extension support to contracting farmers to ensure that production is according to the specification. Skills the farmer learns through contract farming may include record keeping, improved methods of applying chemicals and fertilisers and knowledge of the importance of quality and of the demands of export markets. In view of above, contract-farming arrangements need to be encouraged widely. While doing so, Government needs to protect the interest of both the farmers as well as the industry equitably. This would require arrangement for registration of sponsoring companies and recording of contract farming agreements, in order to check unreliable and spurious companies.

A dispute resolution mechanism need to be set up near to farmers which can quickly settle issues, if any, arising between the farmers and the company under a quasi-judicial manner. The farmers while raising the contracted crops, run the risk of incurring debt and consequent displacement from land in the event of crop failure. Farmers need to be indemnified from such displacement by law.

Model law on marketing has been formulated keeping these requirements in view. This law inter-alia provides for an institutional arrangement for registration of sponsoring companies, recording of Contract Farming Agreement, indemnity to farmers' land and lays down a time bound dispute resolution mechanism.

The Model law has been discussed with the State Governments and the representatives of Trade and Industries at the National Conference of State Agriculture Ministers on 7th January, 2004 and again on 19th November, 2004 and a consensus has been arrived at to give a major thrust to this programme. Several State Governments have already initiated legal amendments to APMC Act. Haryana and Gujarat are among the first States to take steps in establishing an institutional set up for supporting contract farming in these States.

Market Infrastructure

Projections of production and marketed surplus of various farm products show that the quantities, which the marketing system will be required to handle in future, are quite large. A marketing system backed by strong, adequate infrastructure is at the core of agricultural marketing. Market infrastructure is important not only for the performance of various marketing functions and expansion of the size of the market but also for transfer of appropriate price signals leading to improved marketing efficiency. High investment and entrepreneurial skills required for creation and management of modern markets has to come from private sector.

The situation of control by the state has to be eased to facilitate greater participation of the private sector, particularly to engender massive investments required for the development of marketing infrastructure and supporting services. Investment requirement for the development of marketing, storage and cold storage infrastructure in the country during 10th Plan has been estimated by a Task Force to be of the order of Rs. 12,230 crores. The outlay required for the segments is at.

With a view to induce large investment in the development of marketing infrastructure as envisaged above, the Ministry has formulated a scheme for "Development/Strengthening of Agricultural Marketing Infrastructure, Grading and Standardisation". Under this scheme investment subsidy is provided on the capital cost of general or commodity specific infrastructure for marketing of agricultural commodities and for strengthening and modernisation of existing agricultural markets, wholesale, rural and periodic or in tribal areas.

The scheme is reform linked, to be implemented in those States/UTs that amend the APMC Act wherever required to allow setting up of agricultural markets in private and cooperative sectors. The States of Madhya Pradesh, Tamil Nadu, Kerala, Manipur, Himachal Pradesh, Andhra Pradesh, Punjab, Sikkim, Nagaland and Andaman & Nicobar Ilands (U.T.) have so far been notified for implementation of the Central Sector Scheme, being the reforming States. Under the scheme, back ended subsidy @ 25% of capital cost of the project is provided in all States and @ 33.3% of capital cost in case of NE States, hilly areas and SC/ST entrepreneurs.

In respect of infrastructure projects of State Agencies, there is no upper ceiling on subsidy to be provided under the scheme. There is central allocation of Rs. 190.00 crore under the scheme 10th Plan. An amount of Rs. 25 crore has been released under the scheme during 2004-05. Efforts are being made to make the people aware about the scheme through newspaper advertisement, distribution of publicity material and by arranging awareness programmes for officials of States and Banks.

Storage Infrastructure

Storage infrastructure is necessary for carrying over the agricultural produce from production periods to rest of the year. Lack of adequate scientific storage facilities cause heavy losses to farmers in terms of wastage in quantity and quality of produce in general and of fruit and vegetables in particular. It is well known that small farmers do not have the economic strength to retain produce with themselves till the market prices are favourable. There is a felt need in the country to provide the farming community with facilities for scientific storage so that wastage and produce deterioration are avoided and also to enable it to meet its credit requirement without being compelled to sell the produce at a time when the prices are low.

Among the principal agencies engaged in warehousing and storage, FCI constructs godowns for their own needs of procurement and public distribution, the storage of CWC/ SWCs is by and large utilised by FCI, traders and for stocking fertilisers. These principal agencies have, therefore, by and large tended to bypass the requirement of farming community in the rural areas. To consider various aspects of the problems relating to storage of agricultural produce and to improve the country's storage capacity and also storage technology, the Govt. constituted a High level Expert Committee which inter alia recommended that about 20 lakh tonne storage capacity may be created in rural/semi-urban areas.

Creation of storage facilities for agricultural produce, particularly in the rural area has also been emphasised in the National Agriculture Policy. An Inter-Ministerial Task Force constituted by the Ministry of Agriculture has in its report inter alia recommended in 2002 that in addition to

78.83 million tonne available storage capacity in the country additional storage capacity of 130 lakh tonne may be created during 10th plan period. Of this 90 lakh tonne capacity is to be created in private and cooperative sector.

Accordingly the capital investment subsidy scheme titled 'Gramin Bhandaran Yojana' has been launched w.e.f. 01.04.2001. The main objectives of the scheme include creation of scientific storage capacity with allied facilities in rural areas to meet out various requirements of farmers for storing farm produce, processed farm produce, agricultural inputs, etc., and prevention of distress by creating the facility of pledge loan and marketing credit.

Initially scheme was approved for two years i.e. 2001 to 2003. Since there had been huge response to the scheme, it was extended up to 30.9.2004. Beyond this date the scheme has been approved for continuation up to 31.3.2007 with some modifications. Under the pre-revised scheme, back ended subsidy @ 25% of capital cost of the project has been provided. In case of NE States, hilly areas and SC/ST entrepreneurs, subsidy has been provided @ 33.33% of the capital cost of the project. Under the revised scheme, subsidy @ 25% will be given to all categories of farmers, Agriculture graduates, cooperatives & CWC/SWCs. All other categories of individuals companies and corporations would be given subsidy @ 15% of the project cost. In case of NE States/ hilly areas & SC/ST entrepreneurs and their cooperatives, subsidy shall be 33.33%.

Though a total of 90 lakh tonne capacity of Rural Godown was targeted during 10th Plan period, the same has now been revised upwards to 140 lakh tonne on the target of 90 lakh tonne capacity was already achieved during 2004-05 itself. Increased requirement of Rural

Storage has been necessitated on account of increase in the production of food grain and its continuing increasing trend. During last three years 9483 storage projects having a capacity of 141.83 lakh tonne have already been sanctioned under the scheme by now. The capacity-wise break-up of godown are given below:

Capacity-wise breakup of sanctioned project

100-500 tonne	501-1000 tonne	1001-5000 tonne	5000-10000 tonne	Total
5602	1224	2221	436	9483

Out of 9483 godowns sanctioned so far, 335 godowns are in public sector, 2376 are in farmers cooperative, 5050 godowns belong to farmers and 1722 godowns are owned by others like traders, companies, etc. The year-wise physical and financial performance under the scheme has been as under:-

			Financial (Rs. in crores)	
	Target	Achievement	R.E.	Expenditure
2001-03	20	67.35	84.86	84.86
2003-04	27	37.57	80.00	80.00
2004-05	38	36.91	100.00	100.00
2005-06	26	—	80.00	—
2006-07	10	—	35.00	—
Total	121	141.83	369.86	264.86

The scheme has now been made farmers' friendly by allowing subsidy for smaller godowns of 50 MT size in general and of 25 in hilly areas. Five lakh tones capacity to be created is reserved for small farmers and the target of construction in the Tenth Plan is enhanced from 90 to 140 lakh tonne.

Marketing Research

With a view to provide to electronic connectivity to all the important wholesale markets in the country, this Department is implementing a Marketing Information Network Scheme viz. 'AGMARKNET'. The aim of the scheme is to collect and disseminate (price and market related) information in respect of agricultural commodities. The scheme was launched in the year 2000-01 and as on date 1269 markets from all over the country have been linked to a central portal. It is planned to connect 2700 important markets to the AGMARKNET Portal by March 2007.

Price related information: Information on price of agricultural commodities is collected by Auction Officers in the mandi through the process of auction that takes place from early in the morning and goes up to lunchtime. The data is usually sent by e-mail from the mandi in the afternoon indicating the day's minimum price of the commodity, the maximum price and the modal price, i.e. the price at which the maximum sales have taken place.

The quantity of arrivals is also reported. E-mail from all the markets are compiled in the DMI/NIC Headquarter and after verification uploaded on the portal. Information on the portal is in public domain and can be accessed freely. As on date, price information in respect of more than 300 commodities and 2000 varieties are reported on the Site.

Market related information: In addition to price, several other markets related information is provided on the portal. These relate to accepted standards of grades, labeling, sanitary and phyto-sanitary requirements, physical infrastructure of storage and warehousing, marketing laws, fees payable etc. Efforts are on to prepare a national atlas of agricultural markets on a GIS Platform that would indicate the availability of entire marketing infrastructure in the country including storages, cold storages, markets and related infrastructure.

Similarly commodity profiles indicating the post harvest requirements of important commodities in terms of quality, packing, standards etc. are being loaded on to the portal. Commodities already covered include Rice, Bengal gram, Red gram and mustard rapeseed.

Links: The portal has links with several Ministries and Central Institutions that are directly involved in implementing agriculture related programmes. The portal is also linked online with commodity exchanges, providing future prices in respect of cereals, oilseeds, etc. International price trends of agricultural commodities available on FAO website can also be acceded through the portal. The portal is constantly enriched by dissemination of information in regional languages.

Users: Price and other data reflected on the portal is being made use of by several agencies including Banks, Commodity Exchanges, Newspapers, Market Committees, Farmers' Organisations etc. Price information on the portal has credibility since it is generated by the Government system and acts as a reference point.

Technical Support: Technical support to the site is provided by a team of senior officers at the NIC Headquarters at Delhi, State coordinator at the NIC Regional Office and the NIC District Centers located in all districts of the country. Coordination with the State Governments is achieved through the State Marketing Boards under whose administrative control the State regulated markets function.

Financial Outlay: This Department has incurred an expenditure of about Rs.25 crores on the implementation of the Scheme. Outlay for the scheme during 10th Plan is Rs.35 crores.

'AGMARKNET' is a unique live portal on agricultural commodities, technically supported by a high capacity Central server and the programming capabilities of the NIC and the data is fed into the system and later disseminated to farmers in a decentralised mode through the voluntary cooperation of mandi staff.

14

International Trade in Forest Tree Seeds

In the early 1600's, there was international trade on a modest scale in forest tree seed in Europe. During the following century the trade developed remarkably, and considerable quantities of seed, mainly of Scots pine, Norwegian spruce and European larch of central European origin, were widely distributed. Darmstadt in southern Germany became, in the course of a few decades, the most famous center of forest seed trade, and remained so for more than a century. In the eighteenth century, the first extensive forests of coniferous species were planted outside their natural habitat.

At the end of the last century and during the first decades of the present, seed trade in Europe - as far as quantity of seed in the trade is concerned - probably reached its climax. Records of the total annual volume of the trade in that period are not available, but a few examples from private sources give an idea of its dimensions and character. During the winter 1901/02, a single seed firm at Darmstadt received from France and Belgium more than 200 railway truck-loads of Scots pine cones, the seed of which was widely distributed in

Germany and neighboring countries from the Darmstadt-Kiln, simply as seed of "Darmstadt origin". Almost annually during this period several tons of larch seed of alpine origin were sent to various countries: in 1918-1920, more than 4,000 kilograms went from Switzerland to Britain.

Tons of seed of spruce were exported, mainly from the Schwarzwald region in south Germany to Sweden. In 1920-1922, for example, this amounted to 6,000 kilograms. It is also claimed that, in certain years, much spruce seed of southern French origin was exported to Austria and south Germany and there sometimes mixed with seed of local origin for further sale. Increasing quantities of acorns of common and red oak were exported from the Netherlands: during the winter of 1913/14, no less than 120 tons were shipped to a single seed merchant in Copenhagen, Denmark. And many hundreds of kilograms of the fine-grained seed of birch and black alder, the latter now well known for its pronounced climatic races, were collected in Belgium and France and exported via a seed dealer in central Germany, among others, to the same seed firm in Copenhagen, and thence to many widely scattered customers.

Intercontinental trade in forest seed was established in the early days of the eighteenth century, when seed of several eastern American species were frequently shipped to Europe, mainly for use in ornamental plantations. Regular forest plantations of Picea glauca, Pinus strobus, and a few other American species were, however, also raised shortly after 1700 in Europe. The first seed samples of northwestern American species, including Douglas fir and Sitka spruce, were, as is well known, sent to Europe about 1825 by the famous botanical explorer, David Douglas.

Trade on a substantial scale in these species, however, did not begin until after the opening of the Pacific railroad in 1869. The center of the trade in those days was San Francisco, where seed from the northwest was shipped by boat and thence east by train to dealers on the Atlantic coast, or direct to customers in Europe.

Western Canada did not act as an international supplier of forest tree seed until after the first world war. It will be remembered that the Canadian Government after the end of the war shipped, as a gift, seed of Sitka spruce (mainly of Queen Charlotte Islands origin) to war-devastated European countries. Canada, especially British Columbia, is now an important source for seed of various conifers. The first commercial consignments of Japanese larch from Japan to Europe arrived in the second half of the last century.

The first introductions of eucalypts from Australia took place in the early 1800's, mainly along the Mediterranean coasts and in France. Commercial plantations were, however not raised until the second half of the century, and in some of the main eucalypt-planting countries, such as Brazil, not until 1910 or even later. Now some 600,000 hectares have been planted to eucalypts in Brazil.

Picea glauca was introduced into Europe about 1,700 from America and mainly used in shelterbelt plantations, it may be mentioned, merely as a curious fact, that seed of this species has been exported in considerable quantities from Europe (Denmark) to Canada during the last decades. Even seed of such American species as Sitka spruce and Thuja plicata (both, however, of selected origin) have recently been exported from Denmark to American dealers. This is indeed an improved forest seed version of "carrying coals to Newcastle".

Volume of Trade

In most countries there are no official statistical records as to the volume of the import and export of forest seed. Normally, tree seed will be found in the statistical publications under the heading: "Other seeds (mainly horticultural)". However, a few examples drawn from available official and private sources may be mentioned to illustrate the volume of the trade. During the past five years, the average annual import of forest tree seed (with the exception of beech and oak) into Western Germany has been about 27 tons, and is increasing.

The average annual import value amounted to about 850,000 DM. The import value has, however, varied widely from one year to another, depending on the species of seed introduced. During the same period the average annual export from Germany amounted to about 13 tons, the export value being 160,000 DM.

From Great Britain, one of the main forest seed-importing countries, more specific records are available. The British Forestry Commission itself is importing seed, covering its own as well as the main part of private needs. Home collections in Britain usually meet most of the requirements of broadleaved species such as oak, ash, sycamore and beech; but from time to time it is necessary to seek supplies, especially of beech and oak, from continental Europe. Since 1950, the annual import of beech and oak, mainly of southern German and Austrian origin, has varied between zero and almost 30 tons.

The annual import of red oak acorns from the Netherlands was, in the same period, between 10 and 20 tons. For supplies of Scots pine and some of the less widely used conifers, home collections are normally sufficient to provide all requirements. But Sitka and

Norwegian spruce, Douglas fir, Japanese larch, and the other important conifers used in Britain's extensive reforestation and afforestation program must be obtained abroad.

The total annual import of seed of conifers into Britain has varied since 1950 between 5 and 12 tons, the main items being Japanese larch (between 1 and 2 tons from Japan), Douglas fir (1 ton, mainly from the State of Washington in the United States), Sitka spruce (1 ton, mainly from British Columbia), grand fir (800 kilograms, Washington and British Columbia), Corsican pine (500 kilograms, Corsica), lodgepole pine and Norwegian spruce (various origins).

The Forestry Agency of the Ministry of Agriculture and Forestry in Japan has indicated that the average volume of forest seed exported per year from Japan has for the last three years amounted to almost 8 tons, the main species being Japanese larch (about 6,400 kilograms) and Cryptomeria japonica (about 1,200 kilograms). The Netherlands are now the world's main exporter of common and red oak acorns.

For centuries the Dutch people have raised extensive and very beautiful roadside plantations, especially of oak, always selecting in the nurseries for these plantations the plants with the best shape and straightest stems. In spite of the heavy road traffic, most of these often very dense plantations are well maintained, and over-mature trees are replaced with new ones. The trees seed rather abundantly and collection conditions are, as may easily be imagined, generally very good. In certain good seed years hundreds of tons of acorns and beech nuts are exported, mainly to neighboring countries.

However, the annual export of agricultural seed from Denmark alone exceeds 20,000 tons, to the value of U.S. $

12 million, so that it will be realised from these few examples covering some of the main forest seed importing and exporting countries that the volume and monetary value of the international trade in forest seed is relatively quite small.

The importance of international trade in forest tree seed must not, however, be judged solely from statistics. In point of fact, the trade has been, and still is, of considerably greater importance than might be gleaned from the bare import and export figures. In Britain, for example, the Forestry Commission's planting program envisages domestic forests producing, before the end of this century, more than one third of all the timber needed in Britain, the leading European timber-importing country, as compared with only 4 percent in 1938. Such an enormous increase in the national timber production would certainly be impossible without the successful establishment of exotic conifers, originally from introduced seed.

Denmark presents another European example of the successful introduction of numerous exotics. In this country with no native coniferous species of commercial importance, and a forest area comprising only about 9 percent of the total land area, exotic conifers (mainly Norwegian spruce) were introduced on a large scale already in the eighteenth century, and are now planted on 75 percent of the forest area. These intensively-managed plantations (covering 211,000 hectares) are at present supplying more than 50 percent of the Danish softwood requirements, and even allowing an export of certain softwood products.

Furthermore, the Danish beech and oak woods have to some extent been improved in quality through frequent introductions of seed of better races than the indigenous forests of these species. However, the most striking example of successful establishment of an exotic is that of radiate or insignia pine (Pinus radiata) into Southern Hemisphere countries from its very limited area of natural occurrence on the Monterey peninsula of California. It was introduced into New Zealand by the settlers about 1860 and planted mainly for shelter. But as its potentialities for growth became obvious, it was used extensively for planting, with the result that about 228,000 hectares of P. radiata plantations have been established, or over 60 percent of the area for all species planted in New Zealand, and in the near future it is likely to be the country's most important timber.

In the Union of South Africa, in Australia and in the south-central part of Chile this species has also been successfully introduced. In Chile, it extends over well above 200,000 hectares, the annual increment is about 2.8 million cubic meters, and the tree constitutes one of the most important potential raw material resources for the production of pulp and paper in Latin America. Similarly, Pinus canariensis, one of the best pine timbers, has a limited natural occurrence in the Canary Islands, 750 to 2,400 meters above sea level, but has been successfully introduced under a wide range of conditions.

Since 1898, it has been planted on a large scale in the Union of South Africa, as have Pinus patula and various other pines of Mexican origin. Eucalyptus undoubtedly constitutes the best-known exotic in many countries. All the eucalypts important from the forestry standpoint occur naturally only in Australia, but eucalypt plantations covering more than 1 million hectares have been created in various countries lying in world climatic zones of subtropical or Mediterranean type.

On rotations of frequently only 9 to 10 years, they form the basis of very considerable industrial concerns. Most eucalypt species seed early and frequently, and the minute seed is easy to store over longer periods. The Director General of the Forestry and Timber Bureau at Canberra, Australia, has kindly informed the author that, for the last six years, the average annual export of eucalypt seed from Australian Government Departments has been about 62 kilograms and from private suppliers, 15 kilograms, but it is thought that the available figures in the case of private suppliers fall far short of the actual totals.

The Forestry and Timber Bureau at Canberra is now acting as a central clearing house for orders for Australian forest tree seed. Although spectacular results have been obtained with the introduction of eucalypts and radiate pine in several countries, the various northwestern American, European and Japanese species still represent at present a much more important element in international trade in forest tree seed for a large number of countries.

It was recognised already in the early 1800's that Scots pine, the leading European timber in those days, showed considerable variation according to the different seed origins from which the trees derived. Some yielded timber of good, and some of bad, quality for ship building and similar constructional purposes. Some grew vigorously or comparatively well where others failed at an early age.

In 1821, the first provenance trials in Scots pine were hid out, and it soon became evident that there were important racial differences. But not until the early years of the present century, in certain cases not until the last few decades, has any noteworthy attention been paid to the important question of origin of the seed. It was considered foolish not to buy where seed was cheapest.

Accordingly, considerable quantities of Scots pine seed of southern origin were, as indicated earlier, widely distributed simply because such seed was cheaper and frequently of better germinative capacity than seed of local origin in the importing countries. In numerous cases, severe losses were suffered by the forest owners when seed of unsuitable origin had been used. Black alder, with its pronounced climatic races, Norwegian spruce as exported in certain years from Finland and northern Scandinavia to southern countries, European larch of alpine origin, Douglas fir of Shuswap strain as exported to Britain, Denmark and other European countries with similar climatic conditions, and beech nuts collected under badly-shaped but abundantly seeding trees in Holland and various other countries, constitute further examples of indiscriminate and unfortunate seed imports.

Even after the second world war, commercial consignments of European larch of alpine origin have been introduced into countries where it had already long ago been demonstrated that the young larch trees of that origin would be violently attacked by canker (Dasyscypha willkommii). Especially since the 1920's, a mass of evidence has accumulated showing the existence of climatic, form, and perhaps also soil, races within many forest tree species, and it is now generally recognised that seed source in forestry is second in importance only to choice of species for planting projects.

In forestry, it is even more important than in agriculture to use seed of the most suitable origin because of the long rotation normally involved from planting to cutting of the mature trees, and the resultant long time it takes to recognise a possible failure in the choice of seed source. Despite this realisation, international trade in forest tree seed still lacks a foundation of certainty as regards origin of seed, although the trade is improving as buyers are becoming more discriminating.

Several countries, including the United Kingdom, France, Belgium, Switzerland and Western Germany, have passed laws providing restrictions to stop the import of seed of unsuitable origin. The effectiveness of such laws depends not only on the co-operation of suppliers and users, but also on the supervision and inspection of imports. This latter point is rather difficult in many instances because labeling is often inadequate, due to lack of detailed knowledge on the part of the shipper or supplier, as to origin of the seed. Furthermore, in quite a number of commercially important species, our knowledge as to the development of races is still very incomplete.

Merely as a curious example, it may be mentioned that a few years ago several consignments of Douglas fir seed were imported freely simply as "conifer seed" into a country where Douglas fir seed must not be imported without passing a plant disease control. From the above, it should be clear that the widespread use of the forest seed certificate form adopted by the 1951 FAO Conference offers obvious advantages to both suppliers and purchasers of forest tree seed. These certificate forms were the subject of discussion at the 1959 session of the European Forestry Commission, and the Commission felt that now, after 8 years of use, the revision of these forms, which are reproduced here, should be considered. Readers are invited to offer suggestions for such revision.

In most countries the forest seed trade is frequently a state-forest enterprise. However, there are the same advantages in a greater development of private forest tree seed trade as there are in private trade in agricultural seed or in other business enterprises. There are, in fact, some outstanding examples, as in the northwestern region of the United States, of progressive private dealers who have gone a long way toward delimiting specific geographic zones for collection and certification of origin of such important species as Douglas fir, and have succeeded in building a thriving business based on reliable, authenticated, well-tested seed. There would seem to be little doubt that the healthy and successful competition between private and state-enterprise organisations, in countries where these exist, in forest tree seed, must depend on the adoption and careful adherence to a universally acceptable seed certification system.

15

Intellectual Property and Seeds

In developing countries, small farmers dominate food production and using traditional agricultural practices, meet the food requirements of around 66% of the world's population. The introduction of intellectual property rules on plants and seeds under WTO's Agreement on Trade Related Aspects of Intellectual Property Rights (TRIPS) could damage the livelihoods of these 1.4 billion farmers worldwide and undermine food sovereignty and food security.

Before the WTO's Uruguay Round, intellectual property laws were a matter for domestic policy. But the introduction of the TRIPS Agreement made it mandatory for all WTO members to provide for internationally acceptable and enforceable patent protection for new inventions in all areas of technology. For the first time, TRIPS is forcing developing countries to extend intellectual property rights to plant varieties and seeds with consequential impacts on agriculture.

Intellectual property protection as construed under TRIPS could be applied very broadly to allow monopoly rights over individual plant genes and their characteristics. This would imply the removal of farmers' rights over seeds and propagating materials having such genes and characteristics, thus threatening the centuries old practice of saving, using, exchanging and selling farm-saved seed. Patents effectively block competition for 20 years and enable the patent holder to set the market price for the product.

Six multinationals control around 70% of the patents held on staple food crops. The use of patented seeds, plants and genetically modified animals would make small farmers dependent on the corporations that own the patents. In turn, this could lead to fundamental changes in the way agriculture is practiced in developing countries by facilitating the growth of agri-business and the decline of small farms and biodiversity. In addition, if the use of patented seeds became the norm, private corporations would dominate the world's food supply.

International Trade Policies

The biotechnology industry and the development of genetically modified foods is a multi-billion dollar per year industry. According to Merrill Lynch, the market for genetically engineered seeds globally will increase from $450 million in 1995 to $6.6 billion in 2005. Wall Street and private investors liken recent developments in biotechnology to the "discovery of fire." Genetically modified products are hard to avoid; in the United States, sixty to seventy percent of food sold contains some substance developed through biotechnology.

Naturally, with such high stakes, agribusinesses continue to advocate for the stringent patent policies that have been beneficial for them. The Agreement on Trade-Related Aspects of Intellectual Property Rights ("TRIPS"), adopted in 1994, is the controlling international agreement on patent policy, including plant and seed patents. TRIPS, along with other international agreements, monitors whether domestic policy choices of participating nations meet international norms. The TRIPS agreement came out of the same round of GATT negotiations that established the World Trade Organisation ("WTO"), and any nation wishing to participate in the WTO must adhere to TRIPS.

The driving force behind the formation of TRIPS was to curb international abuse of patented technology, infringement, and misappropriations. These issues are at the forefront of the United States' trade policy, as the United States is the world leader in the development of intellectual property rights. Yet, for most of the world, and especially for developing nations, global IP policies as determined by the United States are divergent from national interests and are inappropriate to national infrastructures.

Traditionally, IP and patent policies have struck a balance between individual and societal interests. TRIPS indicates how current international standards do not adequately follow this tradition.

Influence of Business on U.S. IP Policy

Patent policies have historically been enacted to further national interests. Complex national patent regimes, such as those established in the United States, require time and a developed manufacturing infrastructure. Many developing nations' economies are at the same level as the United States during the Great Depression. That is, industrialisation and agriculture are not firmly rooted in the economy. It took the United States 150 years to establish its own complex patent regime. Most developing nations in Africa only attained independence in the mid-twentieth century.

On the other hand, seed businesses have an inherent interest in the potential markets of agriculture-based developing nations. Intellectual property protections imposed through trade are used to protect those markets for these businesses. By imposing patent protections and high licensing fees on new seed products, large seed manufacturers are able not only to capture a large share of the market, but also to earn billions through fees from other organisations. Businesses also use trade to protect their research and development investments abroad.

The development of TRIPS is a perfect illustration of how businesses influence trade agreements. The journey towards TRIPS began in the U.S. private sector a few decades ago. The perceived decline in U.S. competitiveness in the 1970s and 1980s spurred policy trends that focused on restoring U.S. dominance in trade. The lucrative potential of the technology sector brought IP interests to the forefront of the United States trade agenda.

The USTR became a key office in the U.S. government and a lead agency for investment and trade issues in the 1970s. Through this office, private businesses increased their influence on U.S. trade policy. U.S. companies saw success in exploiting influence with the USTR to promote protectionist IP policies abroad. In the early 1980s, CEOs of major technology, chemical, and agricultural companies successfully organised into a powerful lobbying machine.

Under pressure from high-level private sector officials, the USTR began a series of meetings focusing on IP protections with various countries that were viewed as a threat to U.S. IP interests. During the Reagan administration, private sector players had easy access to high level policy developers. Bodies such as the Advisory

Committee for Trade Negotiations ("ACTN"), composed of U.S. business leaders, established official lines of communication between the public and private sector. Following the advice of these committees, the U.S. government focused more on IP as a way to maintain U.S. competitiveness.

The Intellectual Property Committee ("IPC"), composed of major business CEOs, was formed in 1984 to advise the USTR on the IP issues of the GATT agenda. Jacques Gorlin, a private sector consultant for the IPC, authored a paper which became the private sector IP mantra and the basis of U.S. IP policy to this day. The paper focused the United States on three goals for its IP policy: international minimum standards, an enforcement mechanism, and a dispute settlement mechanism. Developing countries were opposed to the inclusion of IP in any international agreements.

One of the most controversial aspects of the Uruguay Round of GATT negotiations was the United States' insistence of IP jurisdiction based on the goals articulated by U.S. private interests. The objection of developing nations was overridden by the developed countries and the Gorlin paper goals were codified in the final TRIPS agreement. TRIPS established minimum IP standards for countries and created an international enforcement mechanism. According to Gorlin, the "IPC got 95% of what it wanted [in TRIPS]."

In 1988, American businesses had another controversial legislative victory with the creation of Section 182 of the Omnibus Trade Act of 1974, more commonly known as Special 301. Dissatisfied with the available international implementation mechanisms at the time, the United States was able to secure, in Special 301, another mechanism for protecting its private industry by allowing it to identify countries that do not provide adequate IP protections. Special 301 then encourages these identified countries to improve their practices.

TRIPS was an overwhelming success for commercial interests, and private industry's aggressive tactics continue to play a major role in U.S. IP policy development. The USTR "has been remarkably responsive to the expressed wishes of these key private sector actors. "In 1998, the USTR stated that TRIPS Council meetings were useful tools to keep developing nations in line with U.S. interpretations of TRIPS.

Post TRIPS Strategy

While many view TRIPS compliance as too much of a burden on the developing world, many businesses see the agreement as too generous. TRIPS provides an extended compliance period for developing nations, which some view as excessive. In addition, TRIPS provides assistance for developing nations in implementing its minimum standards. Article 27 of TRIPS provides certain patent exceptions for agri-chemicals and plants and for public policy, health, and environmental reasons.

While advocates for developing nations say these exceptions will not be very effective, the USTR argued for the stricter exemptions articulated in Ex Parte Hibberd. Because businesses view TRIPS as not going far enough, they have a wellorganised strategy to ensure strict implementation of the agreement. The three main private sector post-TRIPS strategies are: (1) the use of the WTO dispute settlement mechanism, (2) the use of the TRIPS Council Process, and (3) the execution of Special 301.

In order to set strong precedents under WTO IP jurisprudence, industry lobbyists carefully select which infringement cases they will pursue. Since private companies do not have standing under the WTO, they depend on the USTR to bring their suits. A former Counsellor to the USTR said that when filing suits, USTR lawyers work very closely with the counsels of the private parties, i.e. large businesses. This close collaboration has made the United States the most strident enforcer of TRIPS. Through the alliance of the USTR and private industry, the United States has filed more TRIPS complaints than all other WTO countries combined.

The United States has also been uncompromising in its application of Special 301, despite WTO member protests. Special 301, "has done more than any other provision of U.S. trade law to improve the level of worldwide protection of U.S. products embodying copyright. "Yet WTO members protest the use of Special 301 to enforce TRIPS compliance because they believe it exceeded the GATT mandate. Tradė policy is meant to seek compensation when TRIPS is violated and also ensure future compliance. U.S. companies stand to lose billions of dollars a year if TRIPS is not aggressively enforced.

Effects of Current International Policy

TRIPS and similar policies that encourage strong IP protections benefit developed nations. But their effects on developing nations are less obvious. The "North" (the developed Northern hemisphere such as the United States and European Union countries) and the "South" (the developing nations of the Southern hemisphere, including African and Asian nations) are in conflict over the issue. The tropics and subtropics of the South have most of the world's natural genetic resources, yet most patent holders of genetically modified seeds are in the North.

Northern corporations are able to freely acquire Southern genetic resources based on the Southern hemisphere concept of a "common heritage framework" that sees genes as common property. The result is a "one way valve for property claims" - there is an uncompensated exchange of information between the North and South. Northern companies take Southern genetic resources, engineer them to create a patentable seed, and then sell the patented product back to the South. Northern companies claim "natural rights" to protect their information and products. The marketing of the thaumatin plant, an indigenous plant of West Africa, illustrates this point.

Thaumatin is the sweetest substance on earth and has been used for centuries by local villagers in West Africa. In 1993, a patent was awarded to a Korean corporation in partnership with a U.S. university. Billions will be collected by the patent holders from the low-calorie sweetener industry, while West Africa will not receive any of the profits. TRIPS standardised this process of patenting internationally.

The value of the patent is lucrative for the North, but the value of the patent system in the South is controversial at best. First, developing nations bear the enormous cost of systematising foreign patent concepts in their own judiciaries. Secondly, many farmers in the South lack the capital to buy the improved seeds sold to them by the North. Third, Southern seed innovations passed down from generation to generation are not compensated.

Public and Private Partnership

There are roughly 840 million people worldwide who do not receive enough energy through food to live actively.

Many of these people are concentrated is the world's poorest seventy countries. Malnutrition plays a significant role in nearly 12 million deaths per year of children under five. While there are 80 million new people to feed yearly, world grain production growth decreased from three to one percent over the last decade. Genetically modifying technology plays a significant role in food growth and production.

Strong IP protections on the products of this technology are important to foster the development of improved seeds that are resistant to insects, diseases, droughts, and pesticides while increasing crop yield and nutritional content. Yet, in order for these improvements to be effective, products must be made available to the people who need them the most. A balance must be struck between these two diverging interests.

Agriculture and Developing Nations

Agriculture products, staple crops in particular, are a fundamental resource for the poor. Drought, poor soil, plant disease, and political instability all contribute to the dangers of malnutrition and poverty. Genetically engineered seeds potentially have the ability to combat malnutrition and poverty by creating speciality crops with high productivity, better nutritional value, and enhanced resistance to disease. Currently, crop yields in Africa are far below their genetic potential. Grain imports now comprise twenty-five percent of grain consumption in Africa-a dependency that has only increased over the past three decades.

Rising agricultural productivity is directly related to economic growth in developing nations. Agriculture is not only important for producing enough food, but it is key to job creation and employment in most agriculturally based developing nation economies. Small farms are the "engine for progress" in rural areas. In many developing nations, sixty to ninety percent of citizens depend on farming for their livelihood. Developing nations also need to increase agriculture exports in order to spur economic growth. Fair access to trade is therefore fundamental for developing nations.

Trade issues are closely connected to social and economic issues, "policies without immediate economic gain will upset the fragile economic and social balance in developing nations. "Unfortunately, it is not clear developing nations will experience immediate economic gain from TRIPS. TRIPS provisions on genetically modified materials create policies highly unpopular with the populations of developing nations, making enforcement difficult. Resistance to TRIPS has been growing for years in developing nations, some of which has turned violent.

In India in 1998, protesters set fire to Monsanto trial fields during a disobedience operation called "Operation Cremation Monsanto". Following the India protests and similar protests in Bangladesh, farmers in the Philippines staged violent protests at the offices of Monsanto. This additional instability in developing nations is not only troublesome for fragile governments, but also economically detrimental in the long and short term. These reactions also dissuade foreign companies from investing in countries that react violently to their policies and products, thereby keeping valuable capital and jobs out of the country.

Private firms now lead in research and development of GM seeds-a role once dominated by governments and international public institutions. This poses a variety of challenges for developing nations. While the aim of the private sector is to increase profits, the priorities of developing nations are to fight poverty and protect public health. The long-term decline in public sector research diminished the incentives for sharing access and genetic information on newly developed seeds. There is an international movement to increase public sector efforts to create crops that benefit poor farmers.

In order to make this a reality, the private sector must share the latest technological advances with the public sector. The recognition that research must also focus on public needs spurred a number of partnerships in the public and private sectors. The Consultative Group for International Agriculture Research ("CGIAR") is perhaps the biggest player on public seed access on the international front. The CGIAR system consists of sixteen international research centers that focus on staple crops similar to wheat, maize, and potatoes. CGIAR is responsible for the development of "Golden Rice," a vitamin A enriched rice that takes genes from daffodils and micro-organisms.

Vitamin A depletion is a critical cause of malnutrition, and Golden Rice has the potential to save many lives. CGIAR is also an umbrella organisation for other efforts to alleviate poverty and strengthen food security in Africa. The African Rice Center ("WARDA") is funded by CGIAR and based in the Ivory Coast. WARDA encourages partnerships on all levels to increase the productivity and profitability of rice. In particular, they are working on a variety of hybrid rice that combines African genetic traits with productive Asian species ("NERICA"). In trials, use of NERICAs increased productivity by about twenty-five to two hundred and fifty percent.

The Public Intellectual Property Resource for Agriculture ("PIPRA") is another example of a public/private partnership formed to alleviate the difficulties experienced by the public sector in securing access to technologies. The organisation's purpose is to aid "public sector agriculture resource institutions [in] achiev[ing] their public mission by ensuring access to intellectual property to develop and distribute improved staple and speciality crops." PIPRA is working with the USDA and foreign agencies to create an IP asset database of all patented agriculture technologies. This would allow public sector researchers to stay informed about who holds patents and who is currently conducting research.

The Meridian Institute is another non-governmental organisation with a mission to solve problems and conflicts that result from international environmental, health, economic, and social issues. The Meridian Institute hopes to start a dialogue about agriculture issues between policy-makers, industry representatives, NGOs, scientists, academics, and other key players. Efforts such as these demonstrate how strong IP protections can be balanced with the needs of the developing world.

16

National Seeds Policy, 2002

Introduction

Indian Agriculture has made enormous strides in the past 50 years, raising foodgrains production from 50 million tonnes to over 200 million tonnes. In the process, the country has progressed from a situation of food shortages and imports to one of surpluses and exports. Having achieved food sufficiency, the aim now is to achieve food and nutritional security at the household level.

The increase in agricultural production, however, has brought in its wake, uneven development, across regions, crops, and also across different sections of farming community. In the decade of the 'nineties', a marked slackening in the pace of growth has occurred, pointing to the need for infusing a new vitality in the agricultural sector.

Seed is the most important determinant of agricultural production potential, on which the efficacy of other agriculture inputs is dependent. Seeds of appropriate characteristics are required to meet the demand of diverse agro-climatic conditions and intensive cropping systems. Sustained increase in agriculture production and productivity is dependent, to a large extent, on development of new and improved varieties of crops and an efficient system for timely supply of quality seeds to farmers.

The seed sector has made impressive progress over the last three decades. The area under certified seeds has increased from less than 500 hectares in 1962-63 to over 5 lakh hectares in 1999-2000. The quantum of quality seeds has crossed 100 lakh quintals.

The Seeds Act, 1966 and Seeds Control Order promulgated thereunder, and the New Policy on Seeds Development, 1988, form the basis of promotion and regulation of the Seed Industry. Far-reaching changes, however, have taken place in the national economic and agricultural scenario and in the international environment since the enactment of the existing seed legislation and the announcement of the 1988 Policy.

Aims and Objectives

It has become evident that in order to achieve the food production targets of the future, a major effort will be required to enhance the seed replacement rates of various crops. This would require a major increase in the production of quality seeds, in which the private sector is expected to play a major role. At the same time, private and Public Sector Seed Organisations at both Central and State levels, will be expected to adopt economic pricing policies which would seek to realise the true cost of production. The creation of a facilitative climate for growth of a competitive and localised seed industry, encouragement of import of useful germplasm, and boosting of exports are core elements of the agricultural strategy of the new millennium.

Biotechnology will be a key factor in agricultural development in the coming decades. Genetic engineering/modification techniques hold enormous promise in developing crop varieties with a higher level of tolerance to biotic and abiotic stresses. A conducive atmosphere for application of frontier sciences in varietal development and for enhanced investments in research and development is a pressing requirement. At the same time, concerns relating to possible harm to human and animal health and bio-safety, as well as interests of farmers, must be addressed.

Globalization and economic liberalization have opened up new opportunities as well as challenges. The main objectives of the National Seeds Policy, therefore, are the provision of an appropriate climate for the seed industry to utilize available and prospective opportunities, safeguarding of the interests of Indian farmers and the conservation of agro-biodiversity. While unnecessary regulation needs to be dismantled, it must be ensured that gullible farmers are not exploited by unscrupulous elements. A regulatory system of a new genre is, therefore, needed, which will encompass quality assurance mechanisms coupled with facilitation of a vibrant and responsible seed industry.

Thrust Areas

1. Varietal Development and Plant Variety Protection

1.1 The development of new and improved varieties of plants and availability of such varieties to Indian farmers is of crucial importance for a sustained increase in agricultural productivity.

1.1.1 Appropriate policy framework and programmatic interventions will be adopted to stimulate varietal development in tune with market trends, scientific-technological advances, suitability for biotic and abiotic stresses, locational adaptability and farmers' needs.

1.2 An effective sui generis system for intellectual property protection will be implemented to stimulate investment in research and development of new plant varieties and to facilitate the growth of the Seed Industry in the country.

1.2.1 A Plant Varieties & Farmers' Rights Protection (PVP) Authority will be established which will undertake registration of extant and new plant varieties through the Plant Varieties Registry on the basis of varietal characteristics.

1.2.2 The registration of new plant varieties by the PVP Authority will be based on the criteria of novelty, distinctiveness, uniformity and stability.

1.2.3 The criteria of distinctiveness, uniformity and stability could be relaxed for registration of extant varieties, which will be done within a specified period to be decided by the PVP Authority.

1.2.4 Registration of all plant genera or species as notified by the Authority will be done in a phased manner.

1.2.5 The PVP Authority will develop characterisation and documentation of plant varieties registered under the PVP Act and cataloguing facilities for all varieties of plants.

1.3 The rights of farmers to save, use, exchange, share or sell farm produce of all varieties will be protected, with the proviso that farmers shall not be entitled to sell branded seed of a protected variety under the brand name.

1.4 The rights of researchers to use the seed/planting material of protected varieties for bonafide research and breeding of new plant varieties will be ensured.

1.5 Equitable sharing of benefit arising out of the use of plant genetic resources that may accrue to a breeder from commercialisation of seeds/planting materials of a new variety, will be provided.

1.6 Farmers/groups of farmers/village communities will be rewarded suitably for their significant contribution in evolution of a plant variety subject to registration. The contribution of traditional knowledge in agriculture needs to be highlighted through suitable mechanisms and incentives.

1.7 A National Gene Fund will be established for implementation of the benefit sharing arrangement, and payment of compensation to village communities for their contribution to the development and conservation of plant genetic resources and also to promote conservation and sustainable use of genetic resources. Suitable systems will be worked out to identify the contributions from traditional knowledge and heritage.

1.8 Plant Genetic Resources for Food and Agriculture Crops will be permitted to be accessed by Research Organisations and Seed Companies from public collections as per the provisions of the 'Material Transfer Agreement' of the International Treaty on Plant Genetic Resources and the Biological Diversity Bill.

1.9 Regular interaction amongst the Private and Public Researchers, Seed Companies/Organisations and

Development Agencies will be fostered to develop and promote growth of a healthy seed industry in the country.

1.10 To keep abreast of global developments in the field of Plant Variety Protection and for technical collaboration, India may consider joining Regional and International Organisations.

1.11 The PVP Authority may, if required, resort to compulsory licensing of a protected variety in public interest on the ground that requirements of the farming community for seeds and propagating material of a variety are not being met or that the production of the seeds or planting material of the protected variety is not being facilitated to the fullest possible extent.

2. Seed Production

2.1 To meet the Nation's food security needs, it is important to make available to Indian farmers a wide range of seeds of superior quality, in adequate quantity on a timely basis. Public Sector Seed Institutions will be encouraged to enhance production of seed towards meeting the objective of food and nutritional security.

2.2 The Indian seed programme adheres to the limited three generation system of seed multiplication, namely, breeder, foundation and certified seed. Breeder seed is the progeny of nucleus seed.

2.2.1 Nucleus seed is the seed produced by the breeder to develop the particular variety and is directly used for multiplication as breeder seed.

2.2.2 Breeder seed is the seed material directly controlled by the originating or the sponsoring breeder or Institution for the initial and recurring production of foundation seed.

2.2.3 Foundation seed is the progeny of breeder seed. Foundation seed may also be produced from foundation seed. Production of foundation seed stage-I and stage-II may thus be permitted, if supervised and approved by the Certification Agency and if the production process is so handled as to maintain specific genetic purity and identity.

2.2.4 Certified seed is the progeny of foundation seed or the progeny of certified seed. If the certified seed is the progeny of certified seed, then this reproduction will not exceed three generations beyond foundation stage-I and it will be ascertained by the Certification Agency that genetic identity and genetic purity has not been significantly altered.

2.3 Public Sector Seed Production Agencies will continue to have free access to breeder seed under the National Agriculture Research System. The State Farms Corporation of India and National Seeds Corporation will be restructured to make productive use of these organisations in the planned growth of the Seed Sector.

2.4 Private Seed Production Agencies will also have access to breeder seed subject to terms and conditions to be decided by Government of India.

2.5 State Agriculture Universities/ICAR Institutes will have the primary responsibility for production of breeder seed as per the requirements of the respective States.

2.6 Special attention will be given to the need to upgrade the quality of farmers' saved seeds through interventions such as the Seed Village Scheme.

2.7 Seed replacement rates will be raised progressively with the objective of expanding the use of quality seeds.

2.8 DAC, in consultation with ICAR and States, will prepare a National Seed Map to identify potential, alternative and non-traditional areas for seed production of specific crops.

2.9 To put in place an effective seed production programme, each State will undertake advance planning and prepare a perspective plan for seed production and distribution over a rolling (five to six year) period. Seed Banks will be set up in non-traditional areas to meet demands for seeds during natural calamities.

2.10 The 'Seed Village Scheme' will be promoted to facilitate production and timely availability of seed of desired crops/varieties at the local level. Special emphasis will be given to seed multiplication for building adequate stocks of certified/quality seeds by providing foundation seed to farmers.

2.11 For popularising newly developed varieties and promoting seed production of these varieties, seed minikits of pioneering seed varieties will be supplied to farmers. Seed exchange among farmers and seed producers will be encouraged to popularise new/non-traditional varieties.

2.12 Seeds of newly developed varieties must be made available to farmers with minimum time gap. Seed producing agencies will be encouraged to tie up with Research Institutions for popularization and commercialization of these varieties.

2.13 As hybrids have the potential to improve plant vigour and increase yield, support for production of hybrid seed will be provided.

2.14 Seed production will be extended to agro-climatic zones which are outside the traditional seed growing areas, in order to avoid unremunerative seed farming in unsuitable areas.

2.15 Seed Banks will be established for stocking specified quantities of seed of required crops/ varieties for ensuring timely and adequate supply of seeds to farmers during adverse situations such as natural calamities, shortfalls in production, etc. Seed Banks will be suitably strengthened with cold storage and pest control facilities.

2.15.1 The storage of seed at the village level will be encouraged to facilitate immediate availability of seeds in the event of natural calamities and unforeseen situations. For the storage of seeds at farm level, scientific storage structures will be popularised and techniques of scientific storage of seeds will be promoted among farmers as an extension practice.

2.16 Seed growers will be encouraged to avail of Seed Crop Insurance to cover risk factors involved in production of seeds. The Seed Crop Insurance Scheme will be reviewed so as to provide effective risk cover to seed producers and will be extended to all traditional and non-traditional areas covered under the seed production programme.

3. Quality Assurance

3.1 The Seeds Act will be revised to regulate the sale,

import and export of seeds and planting materials of agriculture crops including fodder, green manure and horticulture and supply of quality seeds and planting materials to farmers throughout the country.

3.2 The National Seeds Board (NSB) will be established in place of existing Central Seed Committee and Central Seed Certification Board. The NSB will have permanent existence with the responsibility of executing and implementing the provisions of the Seeds Act and advising the Government on all matters relating to seed planning and development. The NSB will function as the apex body in the seed sector.

3.2.1 All varieties, both domestic and imported varieties, that are placed on the market for sale and distribution of seeds and planting materials will be registered under the Seeds Act. However, for vegetable and ornamental crops a simple system of varietal registration based on "breeders declaration" will be adopted.

3.2.2 The Board will undertake registration of kinds/ varieties of seeds that are to be offered for sale in the market, on the basis of identified parameters for establishing value for cultivation and usage (VCU) through testing/trialling.

3.2.3 Registration of varieties will be granted for a fixed period on the basis of multilocational trials to determine VCU over a minimum period of three seasons, or as otherwise prescribed as in the case of long duration crops and horticultural crops. Samples of the material for registration will be sent to the NBPGR for retention in the National Gene Bank.

3.2.4 Varieties that are in the market at the time of coming into force of the revised Seeds Act, will have to be registered within a fixed time period, and subjected to such testing as will be notified.

3.2.5 The NSB will accredit ICAR, SAUs, public/private organisations to conduct VCU trials of all varieties for the purpose of registration as per prescribed standards.

3.2.6 The NSB will maintain the National Seeds Register containing details of varieties that are registered. This will help the Board to coordinate and assist activities of the States in their efforts to provide quality seeds to farmers.

3.2.7 The NSB will prescribe minimum standards (of germination, genetic characteristics, physical purity, seed health, etc.) as well as suitable guidelines for registration of seed and planting materials.

3.2.8 Provisional registration would be granted on the basis of information filed by the applicant relating to trials over one season to tide over the stipulation of testing over three seasons before the grant of registration.

3.3 Government will have the right to exclude certain kinds or varieties from registration to protect public order or human, animal and plant life and health, or to avoid serious prejudice to the environment.

3.4 The NSB will have the power to cancel the registration granted to a variety if the registration has been obtained by misrepresentation or concealment of essential data, the variety is obsolete and has outlived its utility and if the prevention of commercial exploitation of such variety is necessary in the public interest.

3.5 Registration of Seed Processing Units will be required if such Units meet the prescribed minimum standards for processing the seed.

3.6 Seed Certification will continue to be voluntary. The Certification tag/label will provide an assurance of quality to the farmer.

3.6.1 The Board will accredit individuals or organisations to carry out seed certification including self-certification on fulfilment of criteria as prescribed.

3.7 To meet quality assurance requirements for export of seeds, Seed Testing facilities will be established in conformity with ISTA and OECD seed certification programmes.

3.8 The State Government, in conformity with guidelines and standards specified by the Board, will establish one or more State Seed Testing Laboratories or declare any Seed Testing Laboratory in the Government or non-Government Sector as a State Seed Testing Laboratory where analysis of seeds will be carried out in the prescribed manner.

3.9 Farmers will be encouraged to use certified seeds to ensure improved performance and output.

3.10 Farmers will retain their right to save, use, exchange, share or sell their farm seeds and planting materials without any restriction. They will be free to sell their seed on their own premises or in the local market without any hindrance provided that the seed is not branded. Farmers' right to continue using the varieties of their choice will not be infringed by the system of compulsory registration.

3.11 Stringent measures would be taken to ensure the availability of high quality of seeds and check the sale of spurious or misbranded seeds.

4. Seed Distribution and Marketing

4.1 The availability of high quality seeds to farmers through an improved distribution system and efficient marketing set-up will be ensured to facilitate greater security of seed supply.

4.2 For promoting efficient and timely distribution and marketing of seed throughout the country, a supportive environment will be provided to encourage expansion of the role of the private seed sector. Efforts will be made to achieve better coordination between State Governments to facilitate free Inter-State movement of seed and planting material through exemption of duties and taxes.

4.3 Private Seed Sector will be encouraged and motivated to restructure and reorient their activities to cater to non-traditional areas.

4.4 A mechanism will be established for collection and dissemination of market intelligence regarding preference of consumers and farmers.

4.5 A National Seed Grid will be established as a data-base for monitoring of information on requirement of seed, its production, distribution and preference of farmers on a district-wise basis.

4.6 Access to term finance from Commercial Banks will be facilitated for developing efficient seed distribution and marketing facilities for growth of the seed sector.

4.7 Distribution and marketing of seed of any variety, for the purpose of sowing and planting will be allowed only if the said variety has been registered by the National Seeds Board.

4.8 National Seeds Board can direct a dealer to sell or distribute seeds in a specified manner in a specified area if it is considered necessary to the public interest.

5. Infrastructure Facilities

5.1 To meet the enhanced requirement of quality/ certified seeds, creation of new infrastructure facilities along with strengthening of existing facilities, will be promoted.

5.2 National Seed Research and Training Center will be set up to impart training and build a knowledge base in various disciplines of the seed sector.

5.3 The Central Seed Testing Laboratory will be established at the National Seed Research and Training Center to perform referral and other functions as required under the Seeds Act.

5.4 Seed processing capacity will be augmented to meet the enhanced requirement of quality seed.

5.5 Modernisation of seed processing facilities will be encouraged in terms of modern equipment and latest techniques, such as seed treatment for enhancement of performance of seed, etc.

5.6 Conditioned storage for breeder and foundation seed and aerated storage for certified seed would be created in different regions.

5.7 A computerized National Seeds Grid will be established to provide information on availability of different varieties of seeds with production agencies, their location, quality etc. This network will facilitate optimum utilisation of available seeds in every region.

5.7.1 Initially, seed production agencies in the public sector would be connected with the National Seed Grid, but progressively the private sector will be encouraged to join the Grid for providing a clear assessment of demand and supply of seeds.

5.8 State Governments, or the National Seeds Board in consultation with the concerned State Government, may establish Seed Certification Agencies.

5.9 State Governments will establish appropriate systems for effective execution and implementation of the objectives and provisions of the Seeds Act.

6. Transgenic Plant Varieties

6.1 Biotechnology will play a vital role in the development of the agriculture sector. This technology can be used not only to develop new crops/varieties, which are tolerant to disease, pests and abiotic stresses, but also to improve productivity and nutritional quality of food.

6.2 All genetically engineered crops/varieties will be tested for environment and bio-safety before their commercial release, as per the regulations and guidelines of the Environment Protection Act (EPA), 1986.

6.3 The EPA, 1986, read with the Rules, 1989 would adequately address the safety aspects of transgenic seeds/planting materials. A list will be generated from Indian experience of transgenic cultivars that could be rated as environmentally safe.

6.4 Seeds of transgenic plant varieties for research purposes will be imported only through the National Bureau of Plant Genetic Resources (NBPGR) as per the EPA, 1986.

6.5 Transgenic crops/varieties will be tested to determine their agronomic value for at least two seasons under the All India Coordinated Project Trials of ICAR, in coordination with the tests for environment and bio-safety clearance as per the EPA before any variety is commercially released in the market.

6.6 After the transgenic plant variety is commercially released, its seed will be registered and marketed in the country as per the provisions of the Seeds Act.

6.7 After commercial release of a transgenic plant variety, its performance in the field, will be monitored for at least 3 to 5 years by the Ministry of Agriculture and State Departments of Agriculture.

6.8 Transgenic varieties can be protected under the PVP legislation in the same manner as non-transgenic varieties after their release for commercial cultivation.

6.9 All seeds imported into the country will be required to be accompanied by a certificate from the Competent Authority of the exporting country regarding their transgenic character or otherwise.

6.9.1 If the seed or planting material is a product of transgenic manipulation, it will be allowed to be imported only with the approval of the

Genetic Engineering Approval Committee (GEAC), set up under the EPA, 1986.

6.10 Packages containing transgenic seeds/planting materials, if and when placed on sale, will carry a label indicating their transgenic nature. The specific characteristics including the agronomic/yield benefits, names of the transgenes and any relevant information shall also be indicated on the label.

6.11 Emphasis will be placed on the development of infrastructure for the testing, identification and evaluation of transgenic planting materials in the country.

7. Import of Seeds and Planting Material

7.1 The objective of the import policy is to provide the best planting material available anywhere in the world to Indian farmers, to increase productivity, farm income and export earnings, while ensuring that there is no deleterious effect on environment, health and bio-safety.

7.1.1 While importing seeds and planting material, care will be taken to ensure that there is absolutely no compromise on the requirements under prevailing plant quarantine procedures, so as to prevent entry into the country of exotic pests, diseases and weeds detrimental to Indian agriculture.

7.1.2 All imports of seeds will require a permit granted by the Plant Protection Advisor to the Government of India, which will be issued within the minimum possible time frame.

7.2 All import of seeds and planting materials, etc. will be allowed freely subject to EXIM Policy guidelines and the requirements of the Plants, Fruits and Seeds (Regulation of import into India) Order, 1989 as amended from time to time. Import of parental lines of newly developed varieties will also be encouraged.

7.3 Seeds and planting materials imported for sale into the country will have to meet minimum seed standards of seed health, germination, genetic and physical purity as prescribed.

7.4 All importers will make available a small sample of the imported seed to the Gene Bank maintained by NBPGR.

7.5 The existing policy, which permits free import of seeds of vegetables, flowers and ornamental plants, cuttings, saplings of flowers, tubers and bulbs of flowers by certain specified categories of importers will continue. Tubers and bulbs of flowers will be subjected to post-entry quarantine.

7.5.1 After the arrival of consignments at the port of entry, quarantine checks would be undertaken; which may include visual inspection, laboratory inspection, fumigation and grow-out tests. For the purpose of these checks, samples will be drawn and the tests will be conducted concurrently.

8. Export of Seeds

8.1 Given the diversity of agro-climatic conditions, strong seed production infrastructure and market opportunities, India holds significant promise for export of seeds.

8.2 Government will evolve a long term policy for export of seeds with a view to raise India's share of global seed export from the present level of less than 1% to 10% by the year 2020.

8.2.1 The export policy will specifically encourage custom production of seeds for export and will be based on long term perspective, dispensing with case to case consideration of proposals.

8.3 Establishment and strengthening of Seeds Export Promotion Zones with special incentives from the Government will be facilitated.

8.4 A data bank will be created to provide information on the International Market and on export potential of Indian varieties in different parts of the world.

8.5 A data base on availability of seeds of different crops to assess impact of exports on domestic availability of seeds will be created.

8.6 Promotional programmes to improve the quality of Indian seeds to enhance its acceptability in the International Market will be taken up.

8.6.1. Testing and certification facilities will be established in conformity with international requirements.

9. Promotion of Domestic Seed Industry

9.1 Incentives will be provided to the domestic seed industry to enable it to produce seeds of high yielding varieties and hybrid seeds at a faster pace to meet the challenges of domestic requirements.

9.2 Seed Industry will be provided with a congenial and liberalized climate for increasing seed production and marketing, both domestic and international.

9.3 Membership to International Organisations and Seed Associations like ISTA, OECD, UPOV, ASSINSEL, WIPO, at the National level or at the level of individual seed producing agencies, will be encouraged.

9.4 Emphasis will be given to improving the quality of seed produced and special efforts will be directed towards improving the quality of farmers' saved seeds.

9.5 Financial support for capital investment, working capital and infrastructure strengthening will be facilitated through NABARD/Commercial Banks/ Cooperative Banks.

9.6 Tax rebate/concessions will be considered on the expenditure incurred on in-house research and development of new varieties and other seed related research aspects. In order to develop a competitive seed market, the States will be encouraged to remove unnecessary local taxation on sales of seeds.

9.7 To encourage seed production in non-traditional areas including backward areas, special incentives such as transport subsidy will be provided to seed producing agencies operating in these marginalised areas.

9.8 Reduction of import duty will be considered on machines and equipment used for seed production and processing which are otherwise not manufactured in the country.

10. Strengthening of Monitoring System

10.1 The Department of Agriculture & Cooperation (DAC) will supervise the overall implementation and monitoring of the National Seeds Policy.

10.2 The physical infrastructure in terms of office automation, communication facilities, etc., in DAC will be augmented in a time bound manner.

10.3 The technical capacity of DAC need to be augmented and strengthened to undertake the additional work relating to implementation of National Seeds Policy, implementation of PVP&FR Bill, Seeds Act, Import and Export of Seeds, etc.

10.4 Capacity building, including National and International training and participation in Seminars/Workshops will be organized for concerned officials.

11. Conclusion

The Government of India trusts that the National Seeds Policy will receive the fullest support of State Governments/Union Territory Administrations, State Agricultural Universities, plant breeders, seed producers, the seed industry and all other stakeholders, so that it may serve as a catalyst to meet the objectives of sustainable development of agriculture, food and nutritional security for the population, and improved standards of living for farming communities.

The National Seeds Policy will be a vital instrument in attaining the objectives of doubling food production and making India hunger free. It is expected to provide the impetus for a new revolution in Indian agriculture, based on an efficient system for supply of seeds of the best quality to the cultivator.

The National Seeds Policy will lay the foundation for comprehensive reforms in the seed sector. Significant changes in the existing legislative framework will be effected accompanied by programmatic interventions. The

Policy will also provide the parameters for the development of the seed sector in the Tenth and subsequent Plans. The progress of implementation of the Policy will be monitored by a High Level Review Committee.

Bibliography

Almekinders C. and N. Louwaars, "Farmers' Seed Production: New Approaches and Practices", London: Intermediate Technology Publications Ltd, 1999.

Anon, *Seed Supply. Key Sheets for Sustainable Livelihoods, Service Delivery*, Overseas Development Institute (ODI), 1997

Bramel P., Jones R., Remington T. and C. Longley, "Seed Systems and Disaster Relief: An Overview", Maroko J. and A. Myers, *Planning and Implementing a Seed Fair*, 2002

Cromwell E., Cooper D. and P. Mulvany, "Agriculture, Biodiversity and Livelihood: Issues and Entry Points for Development Agencies", Overseas Development Institute (ODI), 2001.

Cromwell E., *Governments, Farmers and Seeds in Changing Africa.* Wallingford, UK: CAB International. 192 Pages. Available from Oxford University press, 1996

David S. and L. Sperling, "Improving Technology Delivery Mechanisms. Lessons from Bean Seed Systems and Research in Eastern and Central Africa", *Agriculture and Human Values*, 1999

David S., Kasozi S. and C. Wortmann, "An Investigation of Alternative Bean Seed Marketing Channels in Uganda. Network on Bean Research in Africa", *Occasional Publications Series* No. 19. Cali, Colombia: International Center for Tropical Agriculture (CIAT), 1997

de Vries J. and G. Toenniessen, *Seed Systems: Reaching the Poor in Numbers*, Wallingford, UK: CAB International, 2002

Dominguez C., Rohrbach D., Longley K., Momade S. and R. Jones, "Organizing Seed Fairs in Emergency Situations: Improving the Efficiency of Seed Distribution", Patancheru, India: International Crops Research Institute for the Semi-Arid Tropics (ICRISAT), 2001

FAO, "Seed Stocks and Seed Multiplication in Emergency Situations", 1998

Hines D, Wikrema S and L. van Straaten, *Food and Seed Assistance in Recovery from Crisis*, 1998

Jayasinghe U., "Seed Production in the Developing Countries: CIP Strategy", Bogor, Indonesia: International Potato Center (CIP), CIP-ESEAP Region, 2001

Scowcroft W. R, Fiebig W. and V. Bushamuka, "Developing Seed Security Strategies and Programmes for Food Security in Developing Countries", 1998

Sperling L. and D. Cooper, "Understanding Seed Systems and Strengthening Seed Security", *Background paper prepared for workshop on Effective and Sustainable Seed Relief: A Stakeholder Workshop*, Rome: Food and Agriculture Organization of the United Nations, 26–28 May 2003.

Index